TAPPING INTO THE SKILLS OF 21ST-CENTURY SCHOOL LIBRARIANS

TAPPING INTO THE SKILLS OF 21ST-CENTURY SCHOOL LIBRARIANS

A Concise Handbook for Administrators

Audrey P. Church

ROWMAN & LITTLEFIELD
Lanham • Boulder • New York • London

Published by Rowman & Littlefield
A wholly owned subsidiary of
The Rowman & Littlefield Publishing Group, Inc.
4501 Forbes Boulevard, Suite 200, Lanham, Maryland 20706
www.rowman.com

Unit A, Whitacre Mews, 26-34 Stannary Street, London SE11 4AB,
United Kingdom

British Library Cataloguing in Publication Information Available

Library of Congress Cataloging-in-Publication Data Available
ISBN 978-1-4758-1889-5 (cloth : alk. paper)
ISBN 978-1-4758-1890-1 (pbk. : alk. paper)
ISBN 978-1-4758-1891-8 (electronic)

♾ ™ The paper used in this publication meets the minimum requirements of
American National Standard for Information Sciences Permanence of Paper
for Printed Library Materials, ANSI/NISO Z39.48-1992.

Printed in the United States of America

CONTENTS

FOREWORD TO PRINCIPALS

A growing body of research demonstrates that talented school librarians operating in well-stocked, up-to-date school libraries can substantially contribute to student achievement across the whole curriculum. But if you graduated from a typical principal preparation program, odds are that your training never touched on that research. And that's a shame. Audrey Church's *Tapping into the Skills of School Librarians* directly addresses that void. She persuasively describes what your librarian should be able to do for your students, for your teachers, and even for you. Your librarian may well be a potent untapped instructional resource, a resource that you really can't afford to overlook in these days of growing challenges and shrinking budgets.

The book is short and easy to read, but don't be fooled. It is grounded in the research literature and packed with information and practical ideas. Although it offers a vision of what the 21st-century school library and librarian should look like, it's not a book of theories and abstractions. It's a tool. The tone is simultaneously informed and informal. Audrey speaks directly to you as a principal, and *Tapping into the Skills of School Librarians* reads much like a conversation with a knowledgeable colleague.

Perhaps it feels so collegial because—although Audrey has never been a school principal—she has extensively studied how principals operate, the challenges they face, and the opportunities they have. In researching the context in which school librarians work, she has come to understand what principals know and what they *should* know about the librarians who serve in their schools. I don't say this lightly. Audrey's doctoral dissertation was a study of how school principals perceive school librarians. She has continually researched, published, and presented on this subject and on other aspects of principal-librarian relationships over the past decade. As a former high school principal, I am drawn to works by people who grasp a principal's perspective. I believe you also will appreciate that in Audrey's book.

Audrey understands, I think, that most principals are impatient people. Their lives—as the great organizational researcher Henry Mintzberg (1973) once put it—involve a great deal of work, done at an unrelenting pace in an unpredictable environment, characterized by variety, fragmentation, and brevity. She knows your time is precious, and she doesn't waste it. Each chapter in her book plunges directly into the topic at hand, describes what is and what could be, and then offers recommendations and links to resources that can help you maximize the return on whatever you're able to invest in library resources in your school.

As a principal, I particularly appreciate the fact that Audrey acknowledges the human element in the job. Job descriptions for teachers, principals, secretaries, and librarians all look pretty much the same on paper, but they differ greatly in the living. The library media program turns on the quality of the librarian, just as the quality of a classroom experience turns on the quality of the teacher. The notion that any curriculum executes itself or that classes are so intrinsically interesting that it doesn't matter who runs them is more than naive. Librarianship is no more formulaic than administration. You need the right person in the job to realize all the potential packed into your library media program. Audrey rightly argues that stereotypical librarians have no place in today's schools. They must either change with the times or they must be replaced. It's a realistic and refreshing insight, something often missing in books about what libraries and librarians can contribute to student achievement. It's a perspective I think every principal will appreciate.

Mark Twain once observed that the person who *doesn't* read has no advantage over the person who *can't* read. It's not too much of a stretch to say something similar about school principals and librarians. If you're the principal of a school fortunate enough to have a well-stocked library and a talented librarian and you don't use them both, you have no advantage over a principal who doesn't have the same resources—and your students pay the price. This book can help you tap into the myriad ways that a talented librarian might contribute to your school—and I am pleased to recommend it to you.

Gary Hartzell
Professor Emeritus
Department of Educational Administration
University of Nebraska at Omaha

REFERENCE

Mintzberg, Henry. *The Structure of Managerial Work*. New York: Harper & Row, 1973.

PREFACE

Principals are critically important to the work of the school librarian. I know this from my twenty years of experience as a building-level librarian. I know it from my reading in professional journals and from my research, and I know it from the students who are enrolled in my graduate courses in school librarianship. It is the principal who is the instructional leader of the school and who sets the tone and expectations for library use. The principal plays an absolutely essential role in the effective implementation of the school library program.

Given the opportunity a couple of years ago to write an article for *Principal Leadership* on the evaluation of school librarians, I jumped at the chance. When Tom Koerner, vice president and publisher for the Education Division at Rowman & Littlefield, suggested that I might write a book on the topic since it seemed that I might have more to say (a slight understatement, those who know me would suggest), I said yes. I am honored and humbled to write about what librarians do and how they make a difference in student learning.

One of the principals for whom I had the opportunity to work once said to me, "I've never had a librarian like you before." I smiled, took it as a compliment, and said thank you. That statement has stuck with me throughout my career in education, guiding my research and directing my professional efforts. It seems that principals learn what librarians do from the librarians with whom they work. In my role as an educator of future school librarians, I'm ready to prepare them to advocate for their programs and to educate their principals on a daily basis. Maybe, though, just maybe, this book might be of help to the cause.

You principals are busy people. You have much on your plate dealing with students, teachers, parents, community members, central office administrators, school board members, and such. This is a short book and, I hope, an easy read. I hope that it will help you become aware of the tremendous potential that your school librarian has to contribute to your school and that you will take full advantage.

ACKNOWLEDGMENTS

I would be remiss if I did not thank the following individuals for their support, assistance, and inspiration:

- Gary Hartzell, for his willingness to write the book's foreword
- Dr. Scott "Shep" Critzer, Dr. Carrie Mouser Gravely, and Dr. Martha J. Eagle, for reading an early version of the manuscript and providing helpful feedback
- Dr. Judy Bivens, Lori Donovan, Dr. Lucy Santos Green, Carl Harvey, Dr. Becky Pasco, Ken Stewart, Julie Tate, and Steven Yates, librarian friends who suggested supportive administrators
- Priscila Dilley, Dr. David Ellena, Pamela Lumsden, Dr. B. Michelle Maultsby-Springer, and Dr. Beth Niedermeyer, for taking time from their busy schedules to respond to my request for quotations
- Brittany Biesecker and Ashley Currin, for their research on the variety of topics addressed in the book
- Longwood University graduate students who are an endless source of ideas for me as they teach collaborative lessons, including but not limited to (because I am sure I have forgotten someone) Kannan Cangro, Sarah Honaker, Lara Ivey, Yuna Kim, Jenny Larson, Alicia LeRoux, Elizabeth Madigan, and Sara Tatum
- Frances Reeve, Dr. Karla Collins, and Dr. Gerry Sokol, my faculty colleagues
- My mom, who believes in me always; my son Sam and daughter-in-law Alice for their quiet support; my daughter Chelsie, who has

encouraged me word-by-word; and my husband Mike for his infinite patience and understanding

And sincere thanks to the following for their willingness to grant me permission to use their work:

- The American Association of School Librarians and the London-derry (NH) School District: AASL Learning for Life Sample Job Description, Title: School Librarian
- Capstone: *PebbleGo* screenshot
- Kent State University Libraries: *TRAILS* screenshot
- Lara Ivey: Research for Elementary Students digital curation project
- Jennifer LaGarde: May 25, 2015 *Adventures of Library Girl* blog post, "An Open Letter to Principals (Before You Hire a New School Librarian)"
- David V. Loertscher: "The Principal's Taxonomy of the Library Media Program"
- Barbara K. Stripling: Image of the Stripling Model of Inquiry

INTRODUCTION

The purpose of this book is to provide an overview of the various roles of a 21st-century school librarian and to illustrate how, within the context of each role, the school librarian contributes to student learning. Each of the first five chapters contains two sections near the end: research findings relevant to that particular role and a list of additional readings for those who may want to explore that role further.

Chapter 1 addresses the librarian as teacher, exploring the AASL *Standards for the 21st-Century Learner*, various literacies, the inquiry process, the librarian's role in reading comprehension, and student assessment in the library. The positioning of this chapter is purposeful, since the teaching role drives all activities of the 21st-century school librarian.

Chapter 2 addresses the librarian as instructional partner, discussing content curriculum standards and various facets of collaboration from a basic definition to required elements for collaboration to levels of collaboration to models of collaborative teaching. Again, the positioning of the chapter is purposeful, since the most effective instruction by school librarians occurs in collaboration with classroom teachers.

Chapter 3 addresses the librarian as information specialist for students, for teachers, and for administrators. In order to teach in a collaborative instructional partnership, the librarian must be well-versed in various information resources and technologies.

Chapter 4 addresses the librarian as instructional leader, exploring various aspects of this role from within the school (connecting to the school's mission and strategic plan, serving on the principal's advisory council, developing curriculum, promoting reading, serving on the literacy team, integrating technology into instruction, providing professional development for faculty, and modeling professional growth) to the larger learning community. Librarians must serve as instructional leaders within their schools.

Chapter 5 addresses the librarian as program administrator, the behind-the-scenes but very necessary duties of the job. Topics explored in this chapter include collection development, intellectual freedom, access, staffing, the library environment, data, evidence-based practice, and the library's strategic plan. The largely invisible work discussed in chapter 5 provides the foundation on which the four previous roles are built.

Chapter 6 explores the challenges and benefits of working with 21st-century school librarians. Challenges addressed include previous perceptions, librarians of the 20th century, budget and staffing concerns, and the issues of filters and access. Benefits include more accurate performance-based evaluation, the contribution of the librarian in establishing a professional learning community within the school, and maximized student learning. A list of additional readings rounds out chapter 6.

Chapter 7 presents final thoughts and is the only chapter with a subtitle: You have the power! When working with the school librarian or when given the opportunity to hire a new librarian, principals have the power to maximize the library program and the librarian to the fullest possible potential for the benefit of the school community. Principals have the power.

Included in the appendices are a list of state virtual libraries, a "Sample Job Description, Title: School Librarian" from the American Association of School Librarians, and Dr. David V. Loertscher's "Principal's Taxonomy of the Library Media Program."

An index and brief information about the author complete the contents of the book.

1

LIBRARIAN AS TEACHER

"The school librarian facilitates active learning. Librarians work collaboratively with classroom teachers to develop rigorous lessons wrapped in the process skills surrounding core curricula." Pamela Lumsden, Principal, Thomas Dale High School, Chesterfield County Public Schools, VA

School librarians are teachers. That is a plain and simple fact. In perceptions, in discussions, and in staff directories listed on school Web pages, school librarians may be considered "support personnel" or "resource teachers" or "specials," but in fact, school librarians are full-fledged, bona fide teachers in their own right. Consider the following:

- Forty-six states and the District of Columbia require school librarians to hold a teaching license ("Certification" 2015). School librarians are certified teachers who have completed additional coursework to specialize in the field of library science.
- edTPA offers a Library Specialist performance-based assessment for pre-service librarians (edTPA 2015). This assessment requires pre-service librarians to demonstrate competency in teaching and impact on student learning.
- The National Board for Professional Teaching Standards (NBPTS) recognizes school librarians as teachers who can demonstrate teaching excellence based on professional standards (NBPTS 2012). Library Media Early Childhood through Young

Adulthood is one of the twenty-five certificate areas available for National Board Certification.

- School librarians teach individuals, small groups, and complete classes. They teach students, and they also teach teachers, parents, and administrators.

What does this mean for the instructional program of a school? What do school librarians teach?

AASL *STANDARDS FOR THE 21ST-CENTURY LEARNER*

As classroom teachers address *Common Core State Standards* or a state's required curriculum or standards of learning, school librarians address the AASL *Standards for the 21st-Century Learner*. School librarians in the 21st century engage students in learning activities that develop the 4Cs: critical thinking, communication, collaboration, and creativity (NEA 2015). As classroom teachers address content, school librarians address process.

In 2007 the American Association of School Librarians (AASL) published their *Standards for the 21st-Century Learner* which state that "learners use skills, resources, and tools to

1. Inquire, think critically, and gain knowledge.
2. Draw conclusions, make informed decisions, apply knowledge to new situations, and create new knowledge.
3. Share knowledge and participate ethically and productively as members of our democratic society.
4. Pursue personal and aesthetic growth" (AASL 2007, 3).

Each of these standards is further broken down into four strands:

- Skills: "Key abilities needed for understanding, learning, thinking, and mastering subjects"—what students should be able to do (AASL 2007, 8). For example, a school librarian will teach students how to "Find, evaluate, and select appropriate sources to answer questions" (1.1.4) (AASL 2007, 3). With guidance from the school librarian, students investigating the topic of weather can access an online encyclopedia for basic background information about weather and a government Web site for current weather data.

- Dispositions in action: "Ongoing beliefs and attitudes that guide thinking and intellectual behavior that can be measured through actions taken"—mindsets or habits of mind (AASL 2007, 8). For example, the school librarian can encourage students to "Display persistence by continuing to pursue information to gain a broad perspective" (1.2.7) (AASL 2007, 3). Students can explore the weather topic further at the National Weather Service site, http://www.weather.gov. What is the weather like in the city in which they live compared to a city across the country? What is the weather forecast for both cities? Do certain weather patterns emerge?

- Responsibilities: "Common behaviors used by independent learners in researching, investigating, and problem solving" (AASL 2007, 8). For example, the school librarian guides students to give credit when they use the intellectual property of others, to "Respect copyright/intellectual property rights of creators and producers" (1.3.1) by citing their sources (AASL 2007, 3). Students working on weather research are guided to cite sources in their final product, whether it is a report, a brochure, or a presentation.

- Self-assessment strategies: "Reflections on one's own learning to determine that the skills, dispositions, and responsibilities are effective" (AASL 2007, 8). For example, the school librarian will structure learning activities so that students "Monitor gathered information, and assess for gaps or weaknesses" (1.4.3) (AASL 2007, 3). Students will determine when they have adequate information to answer their questions and complete their research and when they need more information in order to complete their assignment.

School librarians in the 21st century structure learning activities in the library to build skills, develop dispositions, promote responsible use of information, and scaffold self-assessment. Working collaboratively with classroom teachers, they teach children to inquire, to construct new knowledge, and to share that knowledge. As librarians address the *Standards for the 21st-Century Learner*, they help students become independent, lifelong learners.

LITERACIES

In order to be an independent learner in the 21st century, an individual must be literate, and literacy today goes beyond the traditional definition of being competent in reading and writing, expanding to competency in speaking, viewing, and listening, and embracing information available in multiple formats. School librarians teach lessons which allow students to become information literate, media literate, digitally literate, and visually literate.

Information Literacy

Information literacy is a "set of abilities requiring individuals to 'recognize when information is needed and have the ability to locate, evaluate, and use effectively the needed information'" (ACRL 2000). School librarians teach children to recognize an information need—from "how do I take care of my pet rabbit?" to "where did Lewis and Clark travel when they explored the West?" to "why did the colonists win the American Revolutionary War?"

Once an information need is determined, students must locate appropriate sources to answer that information need: sources may be print or they may be online. Next students locate the actual information within the source, using an index in a print book or skimming and scanning an online source to zero in on what is needed. Then they must evaluate the information. Does it answer the question? Is it timely, accurate, and credible? Is it sufficient?

Finally, an information-literate person uses that information to answer the identified information need. The answer may be a simple fact, retrieved from the source, or it may require a synthesis of information gathered from a variety of sources, a much more complicated task. School librarians structure learning experiences that allow students to access, evaluate, and use information, and they provide instructional scaffolding throughout this process.

Media Literacy

Media literacy is defined as "the ability to access, analyze, evaluate, and create messages in a variety of forms (print, audio, film/video, Internet, etc.) based on an informed, critical understanding of the nature of mass media, the techniques used by producers of media, and the impact of those techniques on the individual and society" (ODLIS 2014). In order to function effectively in today's society, students must possess media literacy skills.

As citizens in a democracy, they will be bombarded by political campaign slogans, advertisements, and commercials. They must be able to differentiate between fact and opinion and between evidence and inference. They must be able to identify purpose and evaluate bias versus objectivity. Using print political materials, campaign video clips, and candidate and political party Web sites, school librarians provide lessons in media literacy, helping students to analyze the purpose, intent, and validity of the message presented.

Another area in which students must develop media literacy skills is that of consumer economics. Print, audio, video, and Internet messages are designed to sell products: students must learn to be savvy purchasers. From breakfast cereals to the latest toys and games to vehicles to insurance coverage, students must learn to recognize persuasive marketing and advertising techniques. Lessons taught in the library provide students the opportunity to develop a questioning attitude, a critical eye, and the skills needed to make an informed purchasing decision.

Digital Literacy

According to the 2011 ALA Digital Literacy Task Force, digital literacy is defined as "the ability to use information and communication technologies to find, evaluate, create, and communicate information, requiring both cognitive and technical skills." Our 21st-century learners are often referred to as digital natives or millennials, and truly they have not known a time prior to smartphones, wireless Internet, Facebook, and Skype.

A 2015 survey conducted by the Pew Research Center showed that "92% of teens report going online daily with 24% indicating that they are online 'almost constantly,'" and they report using Facebook, Instagram, and Snapchat as their favorite social networking sites (Lenhart 2015). A Web search for "best apps for children" retrieves multiple hits with lists for toddlers, for preschoolers, and for elementary school students. Technology abounds! Yet children are not born knowing how to be ethical, responsible users of information. "Students must be taught to . . . use social tools responsibly and safely" (AASL 2007, 2).

Librarians teach students not only to use information ethically but also to be good digital citizens. They may set up a book review blog where students post reviews and then comment on classmates' reviews, providing the opportunity for authentic writing and for instruction in proper etiquette in posting comments online. They may work with students to create posters or public service announcements discouraging cyberbullying, whether it be by text, e-mail, or chat. They teach responsible and appropriate use of technology.

Librarians also help students to use digital technology for academic purposes. Most students are tech-savvy; they know how to use digital tools for their personal uses. They may not, however, know how to use digital tools to create presentations to share information. School librarians teach lessons on how to use Prezi, Voki, PowToon, ThingLink, WeVideo, and other free Web 2.0 tools. They help students master these tools for academic purposes.

Visual Literacy

Visual literacy encompasses yet another set of skills critical for 21st-century learners. "Visual literacy is a set of abilities that enables an individual to effectively find, interpret, evaluate, use, and create images and visual media" (ACRL 2011). The old adage that "a picture is worth a thousand words" is true. Students are bombarded with images in print, on highway billboards, on television, and online, and they must be taught to read and interpret these images.

Elementary school librarians teach visual literacy skills as they read picture books aloud, discussing and asking students to interpret the illustrations. Using primary source documents such as the images available in the American Memory collection from the Library of Congress, librarians teach children to question what they see. Instruction in reading and interpreting information presented in tables, charts, and graphs offers other chances for visual literacy learning. By including graphic novels in the library collection, librarians provide additional opportunities for students to practice visual literacy skills.

As school librarians teach, the focus of their literacy lessons is to empower students to be information literate, media literate, digitally literate, and visually literate. Students with appropriate skills, dispositions, and responsibilities in these areas will be successful 21st-century learners and citizens.

INQUIRY

If there is one location in the school that should foster inquiry, it is the library! Research begins with questions, and learning begins with questions. Libraries are places of questioning and discovery, places in which questions should be asked and answered.

Questions

One approach to categorizing questions is that of "thick" versus "thin." A thin question is easily answered, many times with a simple "yes" or "no" response, and does not require intense thinking. "In the War Between the States, which side won the Battle of Gettysburg?" is an example of a thin question. A thick question, on the other hand, requires thought and analysis. "Why was the War Between the States fought?" would be an example of a thick question. In lessons taught in the library, librarians encourage students to ask and to respond to thick questions.

Library lessons may also include question brainstorming sessions. In his Questioning Toolbox, Jamie McKenzie suggests the following seventeen categories of questions: essential, subsidiary, hypothetical, telling, planning, organizing, probing, sorting and sifting, clarification, strategic, elaborating, unanswerable, inventive, provocative, irrelevant, divergent, and irreverent (McKenzie 1997). Teaching children to question requires teaching children to think. Students who have the ability to formulate questions in these various categories will have the ability to conduct thoughtful and meaningful research.

Inquiry-Based Learning

School libraries are natural places for project-based learning or inquiry-based learning to occur. "Inquiry-based learning is a complex process where students formulate questions, investigate to find answers, build new understandings, meanings and knowledge, and then communicate their learnings to others" (Alberta Education 2015). School librarians teach children to question, to investigate, to synthesize, and to share what they have found.

In order to help students work through the inquiry process, school librarians may teach them to follow a process model such as Barbara Stripling's inquiry model: As shown in Stripling's Model of Inquiry, students connect, wonder, investigate, construct, express, and reflect. The double-sided arrows in the model demonstrate that this is not a linear process (Stripling 2010).

With inquiry-based learning students begin by connecting to personal interests and background knowledge; they have a question, an issue, a topic that they want to know more about. They work to gain background knowledge in order to provide context for the new information that they will encounter. Working with a K-W-L chart, at this phase of the inquiry process, students are identifying what they know.

Next students wonder; they use their questioning skills to construct both thin and thick questions of varying types. With the K-W-L chart, at

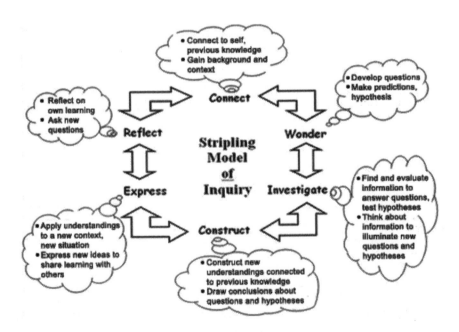

Figure 1.1.   Stripling Model of Inquiry. Reprinted with permission from Dr. Barbara K. Stripling.

this phase they are specifying what they want to know. Wonder is followed by investigation, research, digging for information to answer the questions that have been asked. Next comes the construction stage in which students construct new knowledge and new understandings. Construction is followed by the expression stage in which students share what they have learned (the L portion of the K-W-L chart). Finally students will reflect on both the product that they have created and the process that they have followed, and this reflection may inspire new questions, which causes the inquiry cycle to begin again.

In order for true learning to occur, students must interact with information. Asking questions and following an inquiry process to answer those questions engages learners. Librarians provide instruction and scaffolding as students advance through this process.

READING COMPREHENSION

A traditional role of the school librarian has been to promote books and reading. On a daily basis, librarians work to connect readers with "just the right book." As students gravitate to a particular author or character or especially enjoy a specific genre, librarians will suggest additional books that they might like. The child who loved Jerry Pinkney's wordless picture book *The Lion and the Mouse* may enjoy David Wiesner's *Flotsam*, Eric Rohmann's *Time Flies*, and Henry Cole's *Unspoken*. The reader who loved Avi's *Crispin* may like Kathryn Erskine's *The Badger Knight*.

For those students who are not avid readers, librarians will host reading promotion events to spark interest: book trailers on the morning announcements, a celebration of Dr. Seuss's birthday in an early March Read Across America celebration, or an author visit to the school. Librarians constantly try to find books, authors, or series that will draw less-than-avid readers in. Graphic novels typically appeal to reluctant readers. Boys like books in which the main character is male. Connections can be made between books and movies which are based on them.

Research demonstrates that the more students read, the better they read (Krashen 2004), so a primary task of the librarian is getting reading material in students' hands (or on their device screen). A book, an online article, or a Web site holds no value for the student, however, unless the student can comprehend what is read. While librarians are neither reading teachers nor reading specialists, they play a huge role in helping students develop reading comprehension skills.

> Reading skills involve thinking skills. The extent to which young people use information depends upon their ability to understand what they read, to integrate their understandings with what they already know, and to realize their unanswered questions. To this end, school librarians model and collaboratively teach reading comprehension strategies: assess and use background knowledge, pose and answer questions that are appropriate to the task, make predictions and inferences, determine main ideas, and monitor reading comprehension as well as the learning process (AASL 2010).

Reading Comprehension Strategies

Learning occurs as students connect new knowledge to previous knowledge. The more connections that can be made, the more comprehension and construction of new knowledge take place. One reading comprehension strategy is that of activating or building prior knowledge. For students preparing to read John Boyne's *The Boy in the Striped Pajamas*, library lessons focused on researching the Holocaust can provide critical background knowledge, enabling students to better comprehend the novel.

A second reading comprehension strategy requires visualizing or using sensory images. As students begin a study of the westward expansion, a library visual literacy lesson using photos from the American Memory project can provide mental images of the settlers, their dress, their methods of transportation, and the land on which they are settling. With these images, students can better comprehend the social studies content.

A third reading comprehension strategy involves questioning. Comprehension involves questioning the text and the author. Students reading Andrea Davis Pinkney's *Sit-In: How Four Friends Stood Up by Sitting Down* can learn much about the Civil Rights Movement of the 1960s by asking the following questions: Why is the author telling this story? Who is the author and how has her perspective influenced the telling of the story? How does the author have the characters interact with each other? How does the author use conflict in the story? (Buehl 2013).

A fourth reading comprehension strategy involves making predictions and inferences. The simplest example of predicting occurs in the elementary library as the librarian reads picture books aloud and asks students to predict what will happen next. As the librarian turns the page, the prediction turns out to be accurate or not. Students learn to make inferences based on clues presented in what they read. For example, if the main character in the story describes being outside as part of a crowd of people lined up beside the street, watching elaborate floats go by, the student can infer that the character is attending a parade.

Another reading comprehension strategy involves determining main ideas. Librarians can provide direct instruction on how to determine the main idea as students write brief summaries of books they read for posting on the library blog or in the online catalog. Students must answer the question, What is the book about? These skills can also be addressed in literature circle discussions or book club discussions in the library. In note taking, determining the main idea is a critical skill as students extract the most relevant information.

Yet another reading comprehension strategy is synthesizing. Students must be able to make sense of what they read, use information gathered, and draw conclusions. Note taking and research require synthesis, so librarians will frequently teach lessons addressing this skill. They may focus on students' change in thinking as they move through the process of synthesis, from "I'm thinking" to "Now I'm thinking" to "My new thinking is . . ." They may use graphic organizers to help students extract key concepts, process that information, and then create new meaning.

A final reading comprehension strategy is monitoring and regaining comprehension. Students must be taught to self-check as they read, question their understanding, and make adjustments as necessary. School librarians teach lessons that allow students to practice various fix-it options, from stopping to think to rereading to looking at text features to asking additional questions.

If students are not able to comprehend, they are unable to read for pleasure or for information. The librarian's role in reading instruction is a critical one as she helps students to develop a toolkit of reading comprehension strategies.

ASSESSMENT

What type of assessment will take place in the library? Since the librarian is a teacher, student assessment must occur to determine if students are learning in the library. Is instruction effective, or do adjustments need to be made? According to *Empowering Learners: Guidelines for School Library Programs* (AASL 2009), "the school library program is guided by regular assessment of student learning to ensure the program is meeting its goals" (19). Assessment in the library should be both formative and summative.

Formative Assessment

Since librarians teach process as opposed to content, formative assessment is critical. Formative assessment in the library should utilize a variety of tools: exit tickets (which could be paper-based or online using a tool such as Socrative, SurveyMonkey, or Google Forms); rubrics; checklists; rating scales; graphic organizers; learning logs; reflective journals; conferencing.

Using Stripling's Model of Inquiry in which students connect, wonder, investigate, construct, express, and reflect, assessment to monitor and document student learning should occur at each stage. For example, if students are working to research a topic in U.S. history which interests them, formative assessments might be as follows:

- Connect: At the end of the first class session in the library, an exit ticket on which the specific research topic is stated and the following prompt is completed: I selected this particular research topic because _____. Examination of these exit tickets allows the librarian to (1) determine which students need to work on narrowing their topic, and (2) conference with students who have not provided an appropriate connection for topic choice.
- Wonder: As students move through the wonder stage, they use a Google Form to submit three questions that their research should answer. Examination of the resulting spreadsheet allows the librarian to assess the quantity and quality of questions presented. Students not having the requisite three are required to regroup,

rethink, and resubmit. Those who need additional assistance with quality question creation are remediated.

- Investigate: As students locate sources and begin to access information within those sources, they complete a rating scale to score sources on adequacy on the topic, authority, ease of use, and currency. Total scores indicate to the student (and to the librarian) if additional or different sources are needed.
- Construct: Throughout the note-taking process, students keep a learning log utilizing a three-column format. Column 1 records information found; column 2 records key concepts in the student's own words; column 3 includes any comments or questions the student had. A citation completes each entry. Librarians conference with students, paying particular attention to column 3.
- Express: Students create a final product to demonstrate what they have learned. Prior to submission they self-assess the product using a rubric which includes the various criteria for the assignment.
- Reflect: Students use a checklist to reflect on the process that they followed to find information and to create new knowledge. The final item on the checklist requests that they note any new questions that they have based on their research.

Assessment at each stage allows the student to self-assess and allows the librarian to continuously monitor learning and adjust instruction accordingly.

Summative Assessment

While formative assessment guides student learning and instruction in the library, summative assessment can be used to document overall evidence of student learning. If student scores are higher for quality and variety of sources utilized for a research project following instruction in the library, library instruction has contributed to student achievement.

More formal documentation can be achieved by using an assessment tool such as *TRAILS: Tools for Real-Time Assessment of Information Literacy Skills*, a project of Kent State University Libraries. Using TRAILS, the librarian can administer a pretest addressing the following categories (Develop Topic; Identify Potential Sources; Develop, Use, and Revise Search Strategies; Evaluate Sources and Information; Recognize How to Use Information Responsibly, Ethically, and Legally), provide instruction in the library, and then administer a posttest (TRAILS 2015). Improvement in scores provides evidence of student learning.

RESEARCH FINDINGS ON THE IMPACT OF THE LIBRARIAN AS TEACHER

- According to *Information Empowered: The School Librarian as an Agent of Academic Achievement* (Lance 1999), "the more often students receive library/information literacy instruction in which library media staff are involved, the higher the test scores" (2).
- According to *Report of Findings and Recommendations of the New Jersey School Library Survey Phase 1: One Common Goal: Student Learning* (Todd, Gordon, and Lu 2010), "school librarians in New Jersey clearly do engage in a range of information literacy instruction initiatives. This instruction primarily centers on knowing about the school library, knowing about different sources and formats, with sound levels related to understanding the different strategies in doing effective research, learning how to use the resources, evaluating information for quality, and learning to use information ethically" (147).
- According to *How Pennsylvania School Libraries Pay Off: Investments in Student Achievement and Academic Standards. PA School Library Project* (Lance and Schwarz 2012), "without exception, students are more likely to score Advanced on PSSA Reading and Writing tests where all three educator groups [administrators, teachers, librarians] assess as 'excellent' the library program's role in teaching of all four 21st Century Learner standards" (vii).
- According to *How Libraries Transform Schools by Contributing to Student Success: Evidence Linking South Carolina School Libraries and PASS & HSAP Results* (Lance, Schwarz, and Rodney 2014), "the relationships between student performance on PASS Writing and ELA standards and librarians spending more time teaching information literacy is consistent across a wide variety of student groups,

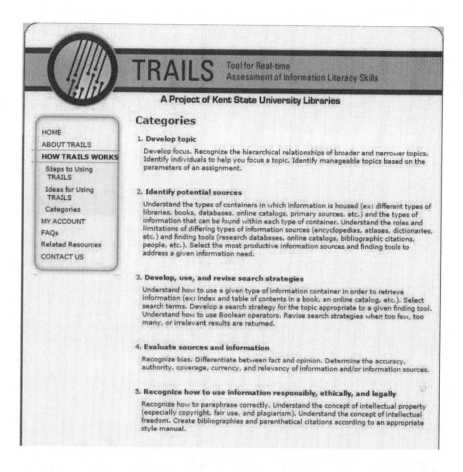

Figure 1.2.   Information-Seeking Skills Categories. Kent State University Libraries (2015). "Categories," TRAILS: Tools for Real-Time Assessment of Information Literacy Skills. http://www.trails-9.org/categories2.php?page=works.

particularly gender, race, disability status, and socio-economic differences" (20).

IN SUMMARY: LIBRARIAN AS TEACHER

School librarians in the 21st century function as teachers within their schools. They provide library lessons which allow students to master the AASL *Standards for the 21st-Century Learner*. They teach students to become information literate, media literate, digitally literate, and visually literate through inquiry-based learning activities. They foster reading comprehension, and they assess student learning. Research findings demonstrate that student achievement is higher in schools where librarians function as teachers.

ADDITIONAL READINGS

Anderson, Cynthia. 2009. "The Five Pillars of Reading." *Library Media Connection* 28, no. 2: 22–25.

Anderson discusses ways in which librarians contribute to reading and literacy instruction in the school.

Butler, Walter. 2014. "Is My Info Lit Program Effective? Answers from Our Assessments." *Library Media Connection* 33, no. 1: 20–23.

Butler describes the framework that he developed for information literacy instruction and assessment for his high school library.

Cooper, Linda Z. 2008. "Supporting Visual Literacy in the School Library Media Center: Developmental, Socio-cultural, and Experiential Considerations and Scenarios." *Knowledge Quest* 36, no. 3: 14–19.

Cooper explores issues that affect the development of visual literacy and suggests ways in which the development of visual literacy can be supported.

Harada, Violet H. 2010. "Self-Assessment: Challenging Students to Take Charge of Learning." *School Library Monthly* 26, no. 10: 13–15.

Harada discusses the power of self-assessment, nurturing self-assessment, and tools that can be used for self-assessment.

Lambusta, Patrice, Barbara Letteri-Walker, and Sandy Graham. 2014. "Rocks in the River." *Knowledge Quest* 43, no. 2: 42–45.

School librarians describe the challenges of implementing an inquiry process model into instruction.

Lewis, Patricia, and Violet H. Harada. 2012. "Did the Students Get It? Self-Assessment as Key to Learning." *School Library Monthly* 29, no. 3: 13–16.

The authors share how they incorporated assessment into teaching practices including a sixth-grade example and a kindergarten example.

Moreillon, Judi. 2014. "Inquiry Learning and Reading Comprehension Strategy Instruction: Processes that Go Hand in Hand." *Knowledge Quest* 43, no. 2: E1–E4.

Moreillon aligns phases of the inquiry process with reading comprehension strategies and notes how they complement each other.

Poinier, Sara, and Jennifer Alevy. 2010. "Our Instruction Does Matter! Data Collected from Students' Works Cited Speaks Volumes." *Teacher Librarian* 37, no. 3: 38–39.

The authors share and discuss data from student work based on instruction in the library.

Schlosser, Maureen, and Barbara Johnson. 2014. "Integrating the Arts through Inquiry in the Library Media Program." *Library Media Connection* 32, no. 6: 8–10.

The authors discuss how they integrated the arts through inquiry projects in their elementary school.

Stripling, Barbara K. 2012. "Inquiry through the Eyes of Classroom Teachers." *School Library Monthly* 28, no. 8: 18–20.

Stripling explores the arc of inquiry, teacher strategies and student skills, and resources and discusses implications for librarians for each.

REFERENCES

ALA Digital Literacy Task Force. 2011. "ALA Connect: Digital Literacy Definition." Accessed May 23, 2015.http://connect.ala.org/node/181197

Alberta Education. 2015. "Inquiry-Based Learning." Accessed May 23, 2015. https://education.alberta.ca/teachers/aisi/themes/inquiry.aspx

American Association of School Librarians (AASL). 2007. *Standards for the 21st-Century Learner.* Accessed May 25, 2015. http://www.ala.org/aasl/sites/ala.org.aasl/files/content/guidelinesandstandards/learningstandards/AASL_Learning_Standards_2007.pdf

American Association of School Librarians (AASL). 2009. *Empowering Learners: Guidelines for School Library Programs.* Chicago: American Library Association.

American Association of School Librarians (AASL). 2010. "Position Statement on the School Librarian's Role in Reading." Accessed May 25, 2015. http://www.ala.org/aasl/advocacy/resources/statements/reading-role

Association of College and Research Libraries (ACRL). 2000. *Information Literacy Competency Standards for Higher Education.* Accessed May 23, 2015. http://www.ala.org/acrl/standards/informationliteracycompetency#ildef

Association of College and Research Libraries (ACRL). 2011. *Visual Literacy Competency Standards for Higher Education.* Accessed May 23, 2015. http://www.ala.org/acrl/standards/visualliteracy

Buehl, Doug. 2013. "Customizing Strategies for Disciplinary Literacy." Accessed May 25, 2015. http://www.wsra.org/assets/Convention/Handouts_2013/a4%20doug%20buehl%20customizing.pdf

"Certification for School Librarians in the 50 States and the District of Columbia." 2015. *School Library Monthly.* Accessed May 25, 2015. http://www.schoollibrarymonthly.com/cert/index.html

edTPA Assessment Areas. 2015. Accessed May 25, 2015. http://www.edtpa.com/PageView.aspx?f=GEN_AssessmentAreas.html

Krashen, Stephen D. 2004. *The Power of Reading: Insights from the Research.* 2nd ed. Westport, CT: Libraries Unlimited.

Lance, Keith Curry. 1999. *Information Empowered: The School Librarian as an Agent of Academic Achievement.* Anchorage, AK: Alaska State Library. Accessed May 25, 2015. http://library.alaska.gov/pdf/anc/infoemxs.pdf

Lance, Keith Curry, and Bill Schwarz. 2012. *How Pennsylvania School Libraries Pay Off: Investments in Student Achievement and Academic Standards. PA School Library Project.* Accessed May 25, 2015. http://lgdata.s3-website-us-east-1.amazonaws.com/docs/2788/580939/PAreport-execsummaryrenum.pdf

Lance, Keith Curry, Bill Schwarz, and Marcia J. Rodney. 2014. *How Libraries Transform Schools by Contributing to Student Success: Evidence Linking South Carolina School Libraries and PASS & HSAP Results.* Accessed May 25, 2015. http://www.scasl.net/assets/phase%20i.pdf

Lenhart, Amanda. 2015. "Teens, Social Media & Technology Overview 2015." Pew Research Center. Accessed May 23, 2015. http://www.pewinternet.org/2015/04/09/teens-social-media-technology-2015/

McKenzie, Jamie. 1997. "A Questioning Toolkit." Accessed May 23, 2015. http://www.fno.org/nov97/toolkit.html

National Board for Professional Teaching Standards. 2012. "Early Childhood through Young Adulthood/Library Media." Accessed May 25, 2015. http://www.nbpts.org/sites/default/files/documents/certificates/nbpts-certificate-cya-lm-assessment.pdf

National Education Association. 2015. "An Educator's Guide to the 4Cs: Preparing 21st-Century Students for a Global Society." Accessed May 25, 2015. http://www.nea.org/tools/52217.htm

Online Dictionary for Library and Information Science (ODLIS). 2014. "Media Literacy." Accessed May 23, 2015. http://www.abc-clio.com/ODLIS/odlis_m.aspx#medialiteracy

Stripling, Barbara. 2010. "Teaching Students to Think in the Digital Environment: Digital Literacy and Digital Inquiry." *School Library Monthly* 26, no. 8. Accessed May 23, 2015. http://www.schoollibrarymonthly.com/articles/Stripling2010-v26n8p16.html

Todd, Ross J., Carol A. Gordon, and Ya-Ling Lu. 2010. *Report of Findings and Recommendations of the New Jersey School Library Survey Phase 1: One Common Goal: Student Learning.* Center for International Scholarship in School Libraries, Rutgers University, July 2010. New Jersey Association of School Librarians. Accessed May 25, 2015. http://www.njasl.info/wp-content/NJ_study/2010_Phase1Report.pdf

TRAILS: Tools for Real Time Assessment of Information Literacy Skills. 2015. Accessed May 25, 2015. http://www.trails-9.org/overview2.php?page=about

2

LIBRARIAN AS INSTRUCTIONAL PARTNER

"There is a strong correlation between high-performing schools and schools who have strong librarians and reading programs. Librarians are a vital part of our campuses. Librarians help establish school-wide programs to promote reading and a love for reading. Librarians are also there to assist classroom teachers supporting the curriculum while providing enrichment activities and opportunities for research."

Priscila Dilley, Director, School Leadership, Fort Worth Independent School District, TX

When the school year begins, classroom teachers anxiously await the release of class rolls to find out who will be in their class for the year. School librarians are teachers without class rolls. As the school year begins, they already know which students will be in their class—every student in the school! That said, librarians do not have the opportunity to work directly with the children unless classroom teachers share.

In an elementary school setting in which the library operates on a fixed schedule, as each class visits on its regular library day, the librarian teaches the students. Typically in secondary schools, and in an elementary school in which the library operates on a flexible schedule, the classroom teacher signs up for library time based on instructional need, and the librarian teaches the students. Whichever situation occurs, it is critical that collaboration take place.

As noted in chapter 1, while the classroom teacher teaches content, the librarian teaches process. Library information skills are most effective when taught, not in isolation, but in connection with what is occurring in the classroom. The librarian, therefore, must serve as an instructional partner who is in full communication with the classroom teacher.

CONTENT CURRICULUM STANDARDS

Knowledge of Curriculum Standards

For several reasons, the librarian must be knowledgeable concerning the content curriculum standards addressed in her school. First she must know content curriculum in order to select and purchase materials for the library collection which enhance the instruction taking place in the classroom. However, she must also know the standards and the curriculum in order to make those key connections between learning in the classroom and instruction in the library.

Additionally, in this age of high-stakes standardized testing and performance-based teacher evaluation, classroom teachers are held accountable for the test scores of students whom they teach. A librarian who is well-versed in the content and skills taught in each discipline at each grade level earns higher credibility with classroom teachers and is more readily accepted as an instructional partner.

An elementary school librarian in a state that has adopted the *Common Core State Standards* knows the kindergarten English Language Arts Standards for Reading: Informational Text, for example, "CCSS.ELA-LITERACY.RI.K.5: Identify the front cover, back cover, and title page of a book," and "CCSS.ELA-LITERACY.RI.K.6: Name the author and illustrator of a text and define the role of each in presenting the ideas or information in a text" (National Governors 2010) and works to address these standards as kindergarten children are in the library.

A middle school librarian knows the grades 6-8 English Language Arts Standards for History/Social Studies such as "CCSS.ELA-LITERACY.RH.6-8.7 Integrate visual information (e.g., in charts, graphs, photographs, videos, or maps) with other information in print and digital texts" and "CCSS.ELA-LITERACY.RH.6-8.8 Distinguish among fact, opinion, and reasoned judgment in a text" (National Governors 2010) and collaborates to plan a lesson with the eighth-grade civics teacher which addresses these standards.

A high school librarian knows the grades 11-12 English Language Arts Standards for Writing such as "CCSS.ELA-LITERACY.W.11-12.7 Conduct short as well as more sustained research projects to answer a question (including a self-generated question) or solve a problem; narrow or broaden the inquiry when appropriate; synthesize multiple sources on the subject, demonstrating understanding of the subject under investigation" (National Governors 2010).

She also is familiar with "CCSS.ELA-LITERACY.W.11-12.8 Gather relevant information from multiple authoritative print and digital sources, using advanced searches effectively; assess the strengths and limitations of each source in terms of the task, purpose, and audience; integrate information into the text selectively to maintain the flow of ideas, avoiding plagiarism and overreliance on any one source and following a standard format for citation" (National Governors 2010) and works with senior English and other content area teachers to collaboratively teach these skills.

In states which have not adopted the *Common Core State Standards*, librarians focus on the specific state standards across content areas and grades levels: the *Alaska Standards* (Alaska 2015), the *Indiana Academic Standards* (Indiana 2015), the *Minnesota K-12 Academic Standards* (Minnesota 2015), the *Nebraska Academic Standards* (Nebraska 2015), the *Oklahoma Academic Standards* (Oklahoma 2015), the *Texas Essential Knowledge and Skills* (Texas 2015), or the *Virginia Standards of Learning* (Virginia 2012).

School librarians are knowledgeable regarding career and college readiness standards, computer and technology standards, and standards across the core disciplines of English, mathematics, science, and social studies. Additionally, since they serve as an instructional partner across all grade levels and all content areas, they are familiar with standards in art, music, foreign languages, theater, health, physical education, even driver's education.

Connection to Curriculum Standards

If a library lesson is to be effective, it is taught in conjunction with content currently being studied in the classroom, and it is taught in collaboration (or at the very least, in communication) with the content-area classroom teacher. Librarians are addressing the AASL *Standards for the 21st-Century Learner* as classroom teachers focus on the content area standards. What might this look like?

Elementary School Example Using Virginia Standards of Learning:

- Students in a kindergarten class have collected and recorded basic weather data for the previous ten days (sunny, hot, rainy, cold, etc.) which addresses "Science K.9 The student will investigate and understand that there are simple repeating patterns in his/her daily life. Key concepts include weather observations."
- They tally the results addressing "Mathematics K.13 The student will gather data by counting and tallying" and create individual graphs "K.14 The student will display gathered data in object graphs, picture graphs, and tables, and will answer questions related to the data."
- In the library they listen as the librarian reads aloud from Lynda DeWitt's *What Will the Weather Be?* (HarperCollins 2002) and discuss predicting the weather, "English K.10 The student will demonstrate comprehension of nonfiction texts. a) Use pictures to identify topic and make predictions." Based on the information they heard and the graphs they have created, they predict what the weather will be for the next several days and add their predictions to their graphs.
- As the science, mathematics, and English *Standards of Learning* have been addressed, the librarian has also addressed AASL *Standard for the 21st-Century Learner* 2.1.3 "Use strategies to draw conclusions from information and apply knowledge to . . . real-world situations" and AASL *Standard for the 21st-Century Learner* 2.2.3 "Employ a critical stance in drawing conclusions by demonstrating that the pattern of evidence leads to a decision or conclusion."

Middle School Example Using Texas Essential Knowledge and Skills

- Sixth-grade students' research focuses on Science "(11) Earth and space. The student understands the organization of our solar system and the relationships among the various bodies that comprise it. The student is expected to . . . (C) describe the history and future of space exploration, including the types of equipment and transportation needed for space travel" (Texas 2010). Students conduct their research using various print and digital library resources.

- The final product for the assignment is in the form of a multimedia presentation, addressing the sixth-grade English "17) Writing/Expository and Procedural Texts. Students write expository and procedural or work-related texts to communicate ideas and information to specific audiences for specific purposes. Students are expected to (D) produce a multimedia presentation involving text and graphics using available technology" (Texas 2010).
- The librarian prepares a pathfinder to guide students to quality print and digital resources, scaffolds students as they gather and synthesize information, and instructs them in the use of various software programs that they may choose to create their multimedia presentations.
- As the science and English *Texas Essential Knowledge and Skills* are met, the librarian incorporates AASL *Standard for the 21st-Century Learner* 1.2.3 "Demonstrate creativity by using multiple resources and formats" and AASL *Standard for the 21st-Century Learner* 3.1.4 "Use technology and other information tools to organize and display knowledge and understanding in ways that others can view, use, and assess."

High School Example Using Common Core State Standards

- Eleventh-graders addressing English Language Arts Standards: Reading Informational Texts: Grades 11-12 "CCSS.ELA-LITERA-CY.RI.11-12.9 Analyze seventeenth-, eighteenth-, and nineteenth-century foundational U.S. documents of historical and literary significance (including The Declaration of Independence, the Preamble to the Constitution, the Bill of Rights, and Lincoln's Second Inaugural Address) for their themes, purposes, and rhetorical features" (National 2010).
- As an introductory activity to provide context, library research focuses on events in U.S. history for the two years preceding the time period in which each of these four documents was written. Students are divided into four groups with each group creating a timeline of at

least five significant events leading up to the writing of the document using an online tool such as Read Write Think's Timeline® or Time-Toast®. Students then share their timelines with the class and describe what they have learned.

- The librarian assists students in finding relevant information and in creating their timelines while addressing AASL *Standards for the 21st-Century Learner* 1.1.9 "Collaborate with others to broaden and deepen understanding" and 3.2.2 "Show social responsibility by participating actively with others in learning situations and by contributing questions and ideas during group discussions."

In each of these scenarios, content curriculum standards were the focus of the lesson. AASL *Standards for the 21st-Century Learner* were integrated into the lesson, and the librarian functioned as an instructional partner, making key contributions to the lesson and to student learning. Successful instructional partnerships require collaboration.

COLLABORATION

Collaboration Defined

"Collaboration is a trusting, working relationship between two or more equal participants involved in shared thinking, shared planning and shared creation of integrated instruction. Through a shared vision and shared objectives, student learning opportunities are created that integrate subject content and information literacy by co-planning, co-implementing, and co-evaluating students' progress throughout the instructional process in order to improve student learning in all areas of the curriculum" (Montiel-Overall 2005). As librarians function as instructional partners, they must be equal participants with classroom teachers in the teaching for learning process.

Through open communication and planning together, teachers and librarians agree upon shared goals and objectives for student learning. They then share teaching responsibilities for the lesson and for evaluating student work. Together they decide if the lesson was successful and, if so, what if any adjustments should be made before they teach it together again: Are additional resources needed? Would the students benefit from more time collecting and organizing information? Should the required student final product be different? If the lesson was not successful, why not? What can be learned from the collaborative experience that might be applied to other lessons?

Required Elements for Successful Collaboration

Successful collaboration does not magically occur. It requires key elements such as partners, resources, communication, time, trust, and a collaborative culture (*Collaborative Teaching* 1997). In order to be an instructional partner, the librarian must have someone with whom to partner. Sound silly? Perhaps, but in this age of high-stakes accountability, classroom teachers have to be convinced that the librarian is an accomplished educator who will help students learn. They have to believe that time spent on instruction in the library is time well spent.

A second component for successful collaboration is resources, both instructional resources and human resources. Instructional resources must be up-to-date, on the appropriate reading and interest level for student use, and adequate in number for the lesson. Human resources must be sufficient for the librarian to have the opportunity to jointly plan, teach, and evaluate: clerical library support staff is critical if the librarian is to function as a collaborative instructional partner.

A third component for successful collaboration is communication. The librarian and classroom teacher must communicate in order to develop shared goals and objectives for the lesson, to jointly plan for the lesson, and to evaluate not only student work but also the lesson itself. Communication can be face-to-face, or it can be technology-enhanced via e-mail, text messaging, or shared documents in a cloud or on the school server.

A fourth component is time—time to plan, time to teach, and time to evaluate. Finding time during the busy school day is always a challenge, and the classroom teacher and librarian may or may not have common planning time; however, time invested in the first iteration of a lesson is time well invested, as subsequent lesson implementations typically build upon the first. Technology can contribute to time savings as well.

The fifth, and absolutely critical, component is trust. As collaborative partners, the classroom teacher and the librarian must trust each other as professional colleagues who will honor and fulfill the commitments to the lesson, sharing the workload, and as accomplished educators who will work for the ultimate goal of increased student learning.

A final component of successful collaboration is a collaborative culture. Partnerships, resources, communication, time, and trust all contribute to a culture of collaboration within a school. An additional key factor contributing to school culture, however, is the tone and expectation set by the building-level administrator. When a principal expects and encourages collaboration to occur, a solid foundation is laid.

Levels of Collaboration

When a collaborative culture exists within a school, the expectation is that collaboration will occur with the ultimate goal of increased student learning. Collaboration occurs at varying levels: cooperation, coordination, collaboration (Forward 2001, 37), and data-driven collaboration (Buzzeo 2008, 28).

At the lowest collaborative level, cooperation, the librarian communicates with classroom teachers, providing resources as needed for classroom instruction. The librarian is perceived as support personnel,

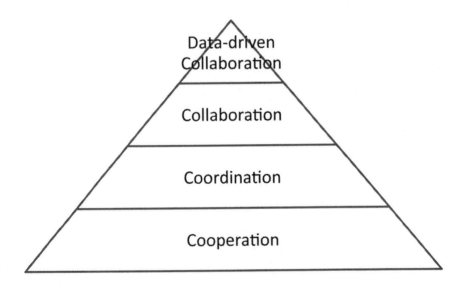

Figure 2.1.   Levels of Collaboration

and there are no common goals for teaching and learning (Forward 2001, 37). Teachers may check out nonfiction books from the library in order to discuss text features (table of contents, index, picture captions, headings, glossary, etc.).

The second level of collaboration, coordination, involves a bit more communication between the teacher and the librarian and connects classroom and library instruction at a basic level (Forward 2001, 37). The teacher alerts the librarian that the students are working on nonfiction text features in the classroom, and the librarian addresses the same content when the children visit the library.

The third level of collaboration, collaboration, as defined earlier in this chapter, involves co-planning, co-teaching, and co-evaluating student work (Forward 2001, 37). The librarian and classroom teacher meet to plan lessons that will take place in both the classroom and the library to address nonfiction text features. They agree that the teacher will address certain elements (picture captions and headings) while the librarian will address others (table of contents, index, and glossary). Assessment will take place in the library as students work with nonfiction texts to identify the various features.

The highest level of collaboration, data-driven collaboration, involves co-planning, co-teaching, and co-evaluating lessons which address identified areas of instructional need (Buzzeo 2008, 28). Disaggregated standardized test data for English Language Arts show that students struggle with nonfiction text features. The librarian and the classroom teacher, working from this data, develop lessons to be taught in the classroom and in the library that focus on these text features. They co-plan, co-teach, and co-evaluate, and they analyze subsequent test data to determine if their collaborative instruction is successful.

Models of Collaborative Co-Teaching

What does collaborative co-teaching between the classroom teacher and the librarian look like? Friend and Cook (2000) offer six models for collaborative co-teaching.

1. One teaching, one observing

In this model, as stated, one educator teaches and one purposefully observes. For example, the collaborative lesson may involve research on famous Americans who contributed to the Revolutionary War effort. On day one of the lesson, the librarian shares quality resources for the project with the students, and the students begin to gather information using graphic organizers. The classroom teacher observes to determine which students are having difficulty locating information at the appropriate reading level and which students are having difficulty extracting information to write on the graphic organizer.

2. One teaching, one drifting

With this model, one educator delivers content and the other educator moves around the classroom or library to assist as needed. The librarian teaches students how to access and search a subscription database such as Gale Cengage's *Health and Wellness Resource Center*. The classroom teacher rotates around the room to guide students as they log in, access the database, and duplicate the librarian's actions.

3. Station teaching

Using this model, the classroom teacher and the librarian work together to create stations and to monitor and guide their use. Students move from station to station to gather information or to complete learning activities. To help students gain background knowledge for reading a novel such as Kathryn Erskine's *Mockingbird*, one station may contain background information about autism; one might contain a YouTube video of an interview with the author; a third might contain links to resources about coping with the death of a sibling.

4. Parallel teaching

When the librarian and classroom teacher parallel teach, a significant amount of co-planning has occurred, and the goal is to improve student learning through a lower student-teacher ratio. As an introduction to a research project on controversial topics, the classroom teacher may present one side of the issue to half the students in her classroom as the librarian presents the other side of the issue to the other half of the students in the library. The two groups switch places and then come together to begin their research and take a side.

5. Alternative teaching

The goal of alternative teaching is to provide students with differentiated instruction and learning activities achieved by dividing the class into appropriate groups. First-graders may be at different skill levels regarding alphabetizing. The librarian may teach the majority of students in the class, working with call numbers for easy books and having students order them as they are found on the shelves by first and second letters of the author's last name. The classroom teacher may work with a smaller group of students who still have difficulty alphabetizing words by the first letter.

6. Team teaching

In a team teaching situation the classroom teacher and librarian are full-fledged instructional partners taking equal roles in planning, teaching, and evaluating the lesson. When teaching a lesson on evaluating sources, the two educators take turns as they walk students, step-by-step, through the evaluation process. For evaluation of a Web site, one discusses the criteria of content; the other discusses the criteria of accuracy; the first discusses the criteria of authority; and so they progress through instruction.

RESEARCH FINDINGS ON THE IMPACT OF THE LIBRARIAN AS INSTRUCTIONAL PARTNER

- According to *How School Librarians Help Kids Achieve Standards: The Second Colorado Study* (Lance, Rodney, and Hamilton-Pennell, 2000), "elementary schools with the most collaborative LM programs average 72 to 76 percent of fourth graders reading at grade level. This is an 18 to 21 percent increase over schools with the least collaborative LM programs" (72); "Middle schools with the most collaborative LM programs average 56 percent of seventh graders reading at grade level. That is an eight percent improvement over middle schools with the least collaborative LM programs" (73).
- According to *How Students, Teachers, and Principals Benefit from Strong School Libraries: The Indiana Study—2007* (Lance, Rodney, and Russell 2007), "across grade levels, better-performing schools

also tended to be those whose principals valued collaboration between LMSs and classroom teachers in the design and delivery of
instruction" (1).

- According to *The Idaho School Library Impact Study-2009: How
  Idaho Librarians, Teachers, and Administrators Collaborate for Student Success* (Lance, Rodney, and Schwarz 2010), "schools at every
  grade level tend to have more students scoring advanced on IRI tests
  and ISAT reading and language arts tests when school administrators
  value more highly, and when teachers and librarians report more
  frequent occurrences of collaboration between teachers and librarians" (3).

- According to *Report of Findings and Recommendations of the New
  Jersey School Library Survey Phase 1: One Common Goal: Student
  Learning* (Todd, Gordon, and Lu 2010), "school librarians in New
  Jersey engage actively with New Jersey Core Curriculum Content
  Standards through a substantial number of cooperations, coordina-
  tions and collaborations. 19,320 cooperations, 11,179 coordinations
  and 3,916 collaborations were undertaken during the 2008-2009
  school year" (4–5).

IN SUMMARY: LIBRARIAN AS INSTRUCTIONAL PARTNER

Librarians work as instructional partners, teaching collaboratively with
classroom teachers to integrate library information skills with classroom
content. Various levels of collaboration may occur from low-level cooperation to high-level data-driven collaboration, and various models of
collaborative teaching may be utilized. Research studies demonstrate
that when teachers and librarians function as collaborative instructional
partners, student achievement is greater.

ADDITIONAL READINGS

Cooper, O. P., and Marty Bray. 2011. "School Library Media Specialist-
Teacher Collaboration: Characteristics, Challenges, Opportunities."
TechTrends: Linking Research & Practice to Improve Learning 55, no.
4: 48–55.

Cooper and Bray address the importance of collaborative instructional partnerships between librarians and classroom teachers.

Donnelly, Andria. 2015. "Getting Started with Collaborative Learning Plans." *School Library Monthly* 31, no. 5: 34–35.
Donnelly addresses the requirements for successful implementation of collaboration between the library and classroom teacher.

Frazier, Dawn. 2010. "School Library Media Collaborations: Benefits and Barriers." *Library Media Connection* 29, no. 3: 34–36.
Frazier discusses the librarian's instructional partner role, the beneficial outcomes for students when the librarian functions as an instructional partner, implementation challenges, and potential solutions.

Freeman, Joanna. Winter 2014/2015. "Beyond the Stacks." *American Educator* 38, no. 4: 32–36. Accessed June 8, 2015. http://files.eric.ed.gov/fulltext/EJ1049433.pdf
Freeman discusses the library as the collaborative hub of the school, various instructional partnerships that can take place, and the importance of connections with teachers and students.

Kimmel, Sue C. 2012. "Seeing the Clouds: Teacher Librarian as Broker in Collaborative Planning with Teachers." *School Libraries Worldwide* 18, no. 1: 87–96.
Kimmel discusses teachers' perceptions of the role of the librarian in collaborative instruction.

Loertscher, David V. 2014. "Collaboration and Co-Teaching: A New Measure of Impact." *Teacher Librarian* 42, no. 2: 8–19.
Loertscher shares his findings regarding the impact of co-teaching (1+1=3) as well as implications from the research for administrators, for classroom teachers, and for school librarians.

Moreillon, Judi, and Susan D. Ballard. 2012. "Coteaching: A Pathway to Leadership." *Knowledge Quest* 40, no. 4: 6–9.
The authors stress the importance of other educators' perceptions that librarians are co-equals to classroom teachers and the benefits effective librarians bring to student learning.

Morris, Rebecca. 2013. "Let's Read It All Together: Developing the Literacy Team." *Library Media Connection* 32, no. 3: 8–10.

Morris discusses various activities and initiatives through which the librarian and classroom teacher can collaborate to promote reading and literacy.

Spisak, Jen. 2014. "Multimedia Learning Stations." *Library Media Connection* 33, no. 3: 6–18.

Spisak discusses what learning stations are, their purpose, the various types, and assessment and feedback.

REFERENCES

Alaska Department of Education and Early Development. 2015. Alaska Standards. Accessed June 1, 2015. http://ok.gov/sde/oklahoma-academic-standards

Buzzeo, Toni. 2008. "Make the Move from Collaboration to Data-Driven Collaboration." *Library Media Connection* 27, no. 3: 28–31.

Collaborative Teaching. 1997 [video]. Lincoln, NE: Great Plains National.

Forward in the Fifth, Berea, Kentucky. 2001. "Professional Collaboration for Information Literacy." In *The Information-Powered School*, edited by Sandra Hughes-Hassell and Anne Wheelock. Chicago: American Library Association.

Friend, Marilyn, and Lynne Cook. 2000. *Interactions: Collaboration Skills for School Professionals.* New York: Addison, Wesley, Longman.

Indiana Department of Education. 2015. "Indiana Academic Standards." Accessed June 1, 2015. http://www.doe.in.gov/standards

Lance, Keith Curry, Marcia J. Rodney, and Christine Hamilton-Pennell. 2000. *How School Libraries Help Kids Achieve Standards: The Second Colorado Study.* Accessed June 8, 2015. http://files.eric.ed.gov/fulltext/ED445698.pdf

Lance, Keith Curry, Marcia J. Rodney, and Becky Russell. 2007. *How Students, Teachers, and Principals Benefit from Strong School Libraries: The Indiana Study—2007.* Indianapolis, IN: Association for Indiana Media Education. Accessed June 8, 2015. http://c.ymcdn.com/sites/www.ilfonline.org/resource/resmgr/aisle/executivesummary.pdf

Lance, Keith Curry, Marcia J. Rodney, and Bill Schwarz. 2010. *The Idaho School Library Impact Study-2009: How Idaho Librarians, Teachers, and Administrators Collaborate for Student Success.* Idaho Commission for Libraries. Accessed June 8, 2015. http://libraries.idaho.gov/files/SchoolLibraryImpactBrief2010505.pdf

Minnesota Department of Education. 2015. "K-12 Academic Standards." Accessed June 1, 2015. http://education.state.mn.us/MDE/EdExc/StanCurri/K-12AcademicStandards/

Montiel-Overall, Patricia. (2005). "Toward a Theory of Collaboration for Teachers and Librarians." *School Library Media Research*, 8. Accessed June 1, 2015. http://www.ala.org/aasl/sites/ala.org.aasl/files/content/aaslpubsandjournals/slr/vol8/SLMR_TheoryofCollaboration_V8.pdf

National Governors Association Center for Best Practices, Council of Chief State School Officers. 2010. "Common Core State Standards." Accessed June 1, 2015. http://www.corestandards.org/ELA-Literacy/

Nebraska Department of Education. 2015. "Welcome to the Academic Standards Website." Accessed June 1, 2015. http://education.state.mn.us/MDE/EdExc/StanCurri/K-12AcademicStandards

Oklahoma State Department of Education. 2015. "Oklahoma Academic Standards." Accessed June 1, 2015. http://ok.gov/sde/oklahoma-academic-standards

Texas Education Agency. 2015. "Texas Essential Knowledge and Skills." Accessed June 1, 2015. http://tea.texas.gov/curriculum/teks/

Texas Education Agency. 2010. "Chapter 112. Texas Essential Knowledge and Skills for Science Subchapter B. Middle School." Accessed June 1, 2015. http://ritter.tea.state.tx.us/rules/tac/chapter112/ch112b.html

Texas Education Agency. 2010. "Chapter 110. Texas Essential Knowledge and Skills for English Language Arts and Reading Subchapter B. Middle School." Accessed June 1, 2015. http://ritter.tea.state.tx.us/rules/tac/chapter110/ch110b.html

Todd, Ross J., Carol A. Gordon, and Ya-Ling Lu. (2010). *Report of Findings and Recommendations of the New Jersey School Library Survey Phase 1: One Common Goal: Student Learning.* Center for International Studies Scholarship in School Libraries. Accessed June 8, 2015. http://www.njasl.info/wp-content/NJ_study/Phase1_ExecSum.pdf

Virginia Department of Education. 2012. "Virginia Standards of Learning (SOL) & Testing." Accessed June 1, 2015. http://www.doe.virginia.gov/testing/index.shtml

3

LIBRARIAN AS INFORMATION SPECIALIST

"Our media specialists are more than librarians. They are a wealth of resources, both print and digital, that do more than help student learning. These educators help create a sense of curiosity and spark self-directed learning in our students."

David S. Ellena, Ed.D., Principal, Tomahawk Creek Middle School, Chesterfield County Public Schools, VA

If there is a traditional role associated with the school librarian, that role would be information specialist. You have a question; your school librarian can help you find the answer. Think reference room or library information commons; think reference assistance, and see the librarian assisting you in finding the best resource to answer your information question. A recent argument, however, has been "since we have the Internet, we don't need librarians any longer." Nothing could be further from the truth.

Where librarians once helped patrons in an information desert, working with print reference books that had been purchased and with *Reader's Guide to Periodical Literature* to locate weeks-old information in print magazines, they now help their students to navigate an online information jungle. Or, as Linton Weeks expressed in the January 13, 2001, *Washington Post*, "In the nonstop tsunami of global information, librarians provide us with floaties and teach us to swim." Librarians are the information specialists in the school as they select, curate, and provide access to quality resources and teach students to use those resources efficiently, responsibly, and ethically.

WORKING WITH STUDENTS

Databases

School librarians are information specialists who provide access to information in paid, subscription database format. Many states offer access to databases appropriate for K-12 students as part of their state digital libraries. For example, students in Alabama can access information from the Alabama Virtual Library searching in Britannica's *Annals of American History* for essays, articles, and primary source documents; in Gale Cengage's *Contemporary Authors* for biographical and bibliographical information about an author; or in EBSCO's *Newspaper Source* for full text access to regional, national, and international newspapers, updated daily (Alabama Virtual n.d.).

Students in Wyoming can access information through *GoWYLD.net: Wyoming's Portal to Knowledge and Learning*, searching in *Britannica School*; in ProQuest's *CultureGrams* for information on countries, states, provinces, and territories; or in *SIRS Discoverer* for information on topics ranging from current events to science to health to technology (Wyoming 2015). Many other states have similar collections of digital resources available for student use. (See Appendix A for a list of state virtual libraries)

However, students must first know that these collections of resources exist and are available for use. To raise awareness, school librarians will model their use during library lessons, or they may feature one a week on the school's morning news show. Secondly, students must know how to access the databases. The school librarian may provide links to them from the school library Web page or send the links out via Twitter from the library's Twitter account. If students need a public library card in order to log in to the resources, in conjunction with the public library, the school librarian might host a library card drive at school.

Finally, students must feel comfortable and confident searching these databases for information. The librarian will provide instruction in their use and require students to retrieve information from them when researching in the school library. In a collaborative lesson with the health and physical education teacher in which students are researching various autoimmune diseases, students may be required to use at least one resource from an academic journal. Gale's *Health Reference Center Academic* might be the database of choice to locate this information. The librarian will walk students through the various search options and show them how to utilize the many useful features of the database—the dictionary, bookmarking, highlighting, noting, and saving to a folder.

Some states do not offer statewide virtual libraries and, even in states where virtual libraries are available, school districts, and sometimes individual schools, will subscribe to additional databases to meet the curricular needs of their students. Since the subscriptions are expensive, the librarian will select and purchase carefully, usually after a free trial subscription during which the product can be explored and used by both students and teachers.

In order to provide additional resources for the social studies department, the librarian may subscribe to one or more of ABC-CLIO's databases such as *American History, American Government, Daily Life Through History, World History: Ancient and Medieval Eras,* or *World History: The Modern Era.* In the areas that their titles suggest, these databases provide access to content (updated daily and aligned to state curriculum and *Common Core State Standards*) as well as primary and secondary sources in a variety of formats (ABC-CLIO 2015).

If the school librarian wishes to provide access to reference e-books, she may select specific titles from Gale's *Virtual Reference Library* (GVRL). When the collection needs a boost in the area of biographical resources and she desires the e-book format which multiple students can access at the same time, titles chosen for high school might be *Top 101 Remarkable Women* (Britannica Digital Learning 2014), *Top 101 World Leaders* (Britannica Digital Learning 2014), or *Newsmakers* (Gale 2015). For middle school, titles selected might be *Making a Difference: Leaders Who Are Changing the World* (Britannica Digital Learning 2015), *Top 101 Athletes* (Britannica Digital Learning 2014), and *Top 101 Musicians* (Britannica Digital Learning 2014).

Virtual reference resources are available for the elementary school library collection as well. The librarian wishing to provide more resources about countries and cultures to allow students to increase their cultural awareness might purchase *World Cultures in Perspective* (Mitchell Lane 2015) or, for general interest and enjoyment, *Everything You Need to Know About Dinosaurs* (DK Publishing 2014), both through the Gale *Virtual Reference Library.*

Students should begin to learn effective online information retrieval skills during elementary school, and databases are available specifically for the younger students. The librarian may subscribe to Capstone Digital's *PebbleGo: The Emergent Reader Research Solution*, providing databases in the following areas: *Animals, Biographies, Dinosaurs, Science*, and *Social Studies*. Primary-grade students can research various animal habitats in the *Animals* database or United States symbols from the American flag to the Liberty Bell to the Washington Monument in the *Social Studies* database and locate grade-appropriate information.

The school district that subscribes to Scholastic's *GO* provides an entire suite of online resources for its K-12 students: for elementary students, *The New Book of Knowledge*; for middle school students, *The Grolier Multimedia Encyclopedia*; and for the high schoolers, *The Encyclopedia Americana. Amazing Animals of the World* intrigues ele-

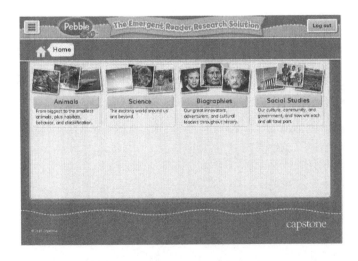

Figure 3.1.   *PebbleGo* Database for Emergent Readers. Excerpted from the work entitled: PebbleGo ©2015 by Capstone. All rights reserved.

mentary school students, while *The New Book of Popular Science* meets middle and high school students' science research needs. For social studies, *America the Beautiful* (elementary to middle) and *Lands and Peoples* (middle to high) provide information resources. *La Nueva Enciclopedia Cumbre* begins to address the research needs of native Spanish speakers.

Whether the databases are available via state virtual library, school district purchase, or individual school subscription, the librarian as information specialist connects students to these resources in order to help them meet their information needs.

Searching on the Web

Of course, students access free information on the Web on a daily basis. It is the librarian's job, as information specialist, to teach them to access it efficiently and effectively, making the most of search tools available to them. At the elementary level, the librarian will teach students to use a child-friendly search tool such as KidRex.org, FactMonster.com, or KidsClick.org.

KidRex.org: Safe Search for Kids, by Kids! offers a very simple search page where children can type their term and retrieve results. Powered by Google Custom Search, searching a term such as "autism" returns numerous, child-appropriate results with reading levels that vary greatly. The librarian would work with students to narrow their search terms, conduct the search, and then access and use information on the appropriate reading and vocabulary level.

FactMonster.com provides not only a search box but also a subject hierarchy so that the student who is searching for information on hurricanes can be taught to either type the word "hurricanes" in the search box or to click first on Science, then on Weather, then on Hurricanes to access both facts on and more articles about the topic.

KidsClick.org is "a web search site designed for kids by librarians—with kid-friendly results." Using it, librarians can teach children multiple approaches to searching—the search box with an advanced search option; a category search where the student drills down through the hierarchy to more narrow subjects; an alphabetical search; a quick search for images, sound, or video; and even a Dewey Decimal search.

A limited number of prescreened sites are returned as results so that the student does not become overwhelmed.

Older students use Google, but they may not use it effectively. Lessons from the librarian can help them learn to narrow and refine their search using the advanced search option found at http://www.google.com/advanced_search. Options include "all these words," "this exact word or phrase," "any of these words," "none of these words" with additional options to limit by language, domain type, file type, usage rights, and other criteria. Students who can manipulate their search terms and criteria have a much better chance of retrieving relevant information. As an information specialist, the librarian will teach students to use appropriate search tools to access needed information.

Evaluation of Information

The librarian as information specialist teaches students to evaluate what they find on the Web. Kathy Schrock (2015) suggests using *5 W's for Web Site Evaluation* asking who, what, when, where, and why. Another set of evaluation criteria includes content, authority, accuracy, currency, and objectivity. The librarian may use Web sites that have been created specifically for the purpose of teaching critical evaluation skills: *All About Explorers, California's Velcro Crop under Challenge*, and the *Pacific Northwest Tree Octopus*. The sites appear legitimate, and critical thinking and critical evaluation skills are needed to discern that they are hoax sites.

It is critical that the librarian teach students to use online databases and virtual library collections when conducting research. It is also critical that students be able to search the Web for information they need and then evaluate what they retrieve. In some instructional situations, however, the purpose of the lesson is not to locate information but rather to work with quality information to meet a research need. In situations such as these, the librarian as information specialist will prepare pathfinders or digital curations of relevant material for the students' use.

Pathfinders and Digital Curations

According to the *Online Dictionary of Library and Information Science* (2014), a pathfinder is "a subject bibliography designed to lead the user through the process of researching a specific topic, or any topic in a given field or discipline, usually in a systematic, step-by-step way, making use of the best finding tools the library has to offer. Pathfinders may be printed or available online."

As librarians partner with classroom teachers for collaborative instruction, they frequently curate resources to create curriculum-related pathfinders that guide students to quality information. Pathfinders may include suggestions for keywords to search in the online catalog or databases, lists of useful nonfiction books in the library collection, and links to appropriate resources found on the Web. These pathfinders may be available in print, on the library Web page, or loaded in a digital curation tool linked from the library Web page.

Halton District School Board (Ontario, Canada) Library Services provide elementary pathfinders on topics ranging from bullying to financial literacy to matter and energy. Students clicking on a topic—for example, multiculturalism—on their Web page (http://www.hdsb.ca/library/pages/elementarypathfinders.html) are taken to a pdf which lists print resources, video resources, catalog subject headings/keywords, and suggested Web sites.

Lewis and Clark Elementary School (Liberty, Missouri) library offers links and pathfinders for each grade level, kindergarten through fifth grades. Pathfinders for kindergarten address beginning computer skills, ants, and worms and insects while pathfinders for third grade address famous Missourians, state study, and astronaut inquiry. Each pathfinder is organized as a LiveBinder (https://lc-lps-ca.schoolloop.com/gllinks).

Pathfinders created for the University of Chicago Laboratory Schools Middle School Library are loaded completely on LiveBinder (http://www.livebinders.com/play/play?id=1603596), labeled as "research hot lists," and link students to useful resources on topics ranging from ancient China to cell biology to the Supreme Court. Colonie Central High School Library (Albany, New York) has used LiveBinders to organize pathfinder resources as pdf files, addressing topics from decades to global world issues to literary criticism (http://www

.livebinders.com/play/play?id=1603596).

Still other schools subscribe to LibGuides to curate and organize resources for students to use. Creekview High School (Canton, Georgia) offers curations on a variety of research assignment–related topics from conspiracy theories to dehumanization to the Harlem Renaissance (http://creekview.libguides.com/index.php). Within their LibGuides, Thomas Dale High School West Campus Library (Chester, Virginia) organizes their pathfinders by content area for easy student access, from the persuasive essay under English to business of the gods under Latin to life cycle of the stars under science (http://libguides.ccpsnet .net/tdhs/west/pathfinders).

Whatever the format—print, pdf, LiveBinder, LibGuide—the purpose is the same: to provide students with ready access to information in quality resources to meet their information need. As the information specialist in the school, the librarian connects students to relevant information.

Intellectual Property

As the librarian facilitates access to information, she constantly emphasizes to students the concept of intellectual property, of giving credit where credit is due. As students research in the library, she provides lessons and scaffolding for note taking, paraphrasing, and synthesizing information to create the final product, whatever it may be—a written report, an oral presentation, a Prezi, a PowerPoint, or a PowToon. She also provides instruction and scaffolding for citation of sources.

Beginning in elementary school, students should be taught how to (and should be expected to) cite their sources. Obviously first-graders will not cite in MLA or APA format. That said, when using encyclopedias, they can cite the name of the article and the name of the encyclopedia where their information was found; upper elementary students can give author, title of article, title of encyclopedia, publication date, and, if online, date of access (Schrock n.d.). As students move to middle and high school, more formal citations should be required.

Gone are the days when students have to painstakingly build citations, word by word, punctuation element by punctuation element. As information specialist, the librarian will provide access to online citation tools. Students learning to cite or needing significant assistance in building citations and reference lists may use one of the following free tools:

- BibMe (http://bibme.org) allows students to create citations in APA, Chicago, MLA, and many other styles
- Citation Machine (http://www.citationmachine.net) allows students to create citations in APA, Chicago, MLA, and Turabian formats
- CiteFast (http://www.citefast.com) allows students to create citations in APA, Chicago, and MLA formats
- EasyBib (http://www.easybib.com) allows students to create MLA citations for free with upgrades available for APA, Chicago, and other styles
- Zotero (http://www.zotero.org) offers more of a research suite, allowing students to gather, organize, and cite information using various styles

Some school districts subscribe to research suites such as Noodle-Tools (http://noodletools.com). Using NoodleTools Express, students can create one or two citations in MLA, APA, or Chicago format for free, but NoodleTools Premium provides "integrated tools for note-taking, outlining, citation, document archiving/annotation, and collaborative research and writing" (NoodleTools n.d.).

For those students more proficient with citing sources and creating reference lists, the librarian will guide them to the Purdue Online Writing Lab (OWL), where they can find information and examples for APA, Chicago, and MLA formats (https://owl.english.purdue.edu/owl/section/2/). The critical concept is that of intellectual property and crediting the work of others for the use of their intellectual property. As an information specialist, the librarian works to make sure that students fully understand this concept and that the crediting of others becomes a given, a natural and automatic part of the research process.

Presentation Tools

Just as students must no longer struggle comma by comma and period by period in constructing citations, no longer must their final product be a written report. Web 2.0 tools abound, and the librarian (perhaps in partnership with the instructional technology resource teacher/computer teacher/technology integrator) guides students in the use of these tools.

- A boring, traditional vocabulary lesson can become interactive as students use an online dictionary site to look up a vocabulary word, rewrite the definition in their own words, and post it to a common Padlet wall (http://www.padlet.com). The saved wall becomes the class vocabulary list for the week.
- Students who are shy speaking in front of others can make oral presentations in class using Voki (http://www.voki.com), creating and customizing a speaking character, recording their voice, publishing, and sharing.
- Students can use PowToon (http://www.powtoon.com) to create animated Web-based presentations, writing their script, recording the voiceover, and adding visuals. Possible applications across content areas are endless.
- True synthesis of information is required when students must create an infographic as their final product for an assignment. Popular creation tools include Easel.ly (http://www.easel.ly), Canva (http://www.canva.com), and Piktochart (http://piktochart .com).
- Perhaps the final learning outcome for an assignment is a timeline created using TimeToast (http://www.timetoast.com) or a graphic organizer showing the relationship of various concepts created using Popplet (http://popplet.com).

When students have the opportunity to use alternative formats to present their final product, they are more fully engaged in the learning process. Learners in the 21st century must be able to utilize technology tools effectively to present information. The librarian guides them through this process.

Digital Citizenship

As students access, gather, evaluate, organize, and share information, they must do so within the overall context of digital citizenship. The International Society for Technology in Education (ISTE 2007) defines

Figure 3.2.   Research Symbaloo for Elementary School Students. Reprinted with permission from Lara Ivey.

digital citizenship: "Students understand human, cultural, and societal issues related to technology and practice legal and ethical behavior." DigitalCitizenship.net (2015) provides the following definition: "Digital citizenship is the norms of appropriate, responsible technology use." The Global Digital Citizen Foundation (2015) emphasizes responsibility and respect for oneself, for others, and for property.

In the 21st century, then, digital citizenship is a complicated concept that includes but goes beyond Internet safety. It includes but goes beyond intellectual property and citation. It involves both respect and responsibility; it involves relationships among digital users; and it involves relationships between the user and the technology/information. It involves both consuming and producing information. As an information specialist, the librarian will work with classroom teachers to help students understand what is involved in digital citizenship and to help students grow into that citizenship.

INFORMATION SPECIALIST FOR TEACHERS

The librarian works as a colleague, fellow teacher, and instructional partner with classroom teachers; however, she also serves as an information specialist for them. She provides access to resources that can greatly enhance their teaching:

- She may share a cool tool or Web site that she discovers, such as Newsela (http://newsela.com), which provides access to current news articles with adjustable Lexile levels, facilitating differentiation as students can read the same content on different reading levels.
- She may provide access to teaching resources such as the printable student handouts and other materials available at Plagiarism.org (http://www.plagiarism.org/resources/student-materials) or the huge variety of graphic organizer tools collected and shared at the CCHS Resource Center "Organization Station" tab at http://www.livebinders.com/play/play?id=405506.
- When the school district embraces project-based learning, adopts a BYOD/BYOT policy, or purchases Chromebooks for every student, she may organize and curate information and resources about that issue so that teachers can be better informed.

Additionally the librarian may provide professional development workshops for teachers in the use of subscription databases relevant to their grade level or content area or in the use of one of the Web 2.0 tools the teacher wants to try with his students. Librarians serve as information specialists, not only for students but also for their teacher colleagues.

INFORMATION SPECIALIST FOR ADMINISTRATORS

Administrators need information too, and librarians are information specialists. What does a flipped classroom look like in a K-12 environment? What's involved in creating a makerspace? How does project-based learning affect student standardized test scores? Inquiring administrators want to know, and librarians can find the answers.

- At a recent conference, a presenter referenced a particular journal article, and the principal would like to read it. The librarian retrieves it full text from ERIC (http://eric.ed.gov) as a pdf file, and it arrives in the principal's e-mail a couple of hours later.

- Taking a doctoral course and in need of a certain dissertation? The librarian locates it in the digital commons of the sponsoring university, downloads the pdf, and e-mails it to the principal.
- A certain motivational speaker is under consideration as the keynote for next school year's opening convocation, and the superintendent wants recommendations. The librarian shares a video of a previous presentation that she located online and searches various social media sites for reviews of prior presentations.

Librarians are information specialists for administrators as well.

RESEARCH FINDINGS ON THE IMPACT OF THE LIBRARIAN AS INFORMATION SPECIALIST

- According to *Student Learning through Ohio School Libraries* (Todd and Kuhlthau 2004), "89.6% of the students indicate that the school library has helped them search the Internet better . . . explicit and systematic teaching of internet searching and research strategies is a key mechanism in this help, both at an individual and class level. Perhaps more importantly, the school library plays a critical role in enabling students to be more careful with finding internet information" (11).
- According to *Student Learning through Wisconsin School Library Media Centers: Case Study Report* (Smith 2006), "the LMS has a more direct impact on students' performance. The program gives students research and information technology tools and skills that they can use in all content areas. It develops their critical thinking ability and opens their eyes to a wide range of resources and information" (7).
- According to *The Idaho School Library Impact Study-2009: How Idaho Librarians, Teachers, and Administrators Collaborate for Student Success* (Lance, Rodney, and Schwarz 2010), "where principals and other administrators rated the teaching of ICT standards as excellent, students at all three grade levels—elementary, middle and high school—were consistently more likely to earn advanced scores on the ISAT reading and language arts tests" (9).

IN SUMMARY: LIBRARIAN AS INFORMATION SPECIALIST

School librarians in the 21st century function as information specialists
within their schools. They provide students with access to subscription
databases. They teach students how to search the Web effectively, how
to evaluate the information located, and how to cite sources used. They
curate quality resources, prepare pathfinders, and promote digital citizenship. They teach students to use various presentation tools, provide
resources and professional development for fellow teachers, and serve
as information specialists for their administrators. Research findings
demonstrate that student achievement is higher in schools where librarians function as information specialists.

ADDITIONAL READINGS

Harris, Frances Jacobsen. 2011. "The School Librarian as Information
Specialist: A Vibrant Species." *Knowledge Quest* 39, no. 5: 28–32.
    Harris explores the role of the school librarian as information spe-
cialist, teaching students to evaluate information found on the Web and
to be responsible digital citizens.

Howard, Jody K. 2010. "Information Specialist and Leader: Taking on
Collection and Curriculum Mapping." *School Library Monthly* 27, no.
1: 35–37.
    Howard asserts that the librarian must be an information specialist
to align the collection with the curriculum and ensure that teachers and
students have the resources needed for teaching and for learning.

Johnston, Melissa P. 2013. "Taking the Lead with Technology Integration." *School Library Monthly* 29, no. 4: 33–35.
    Johnston discusses how the librarian integrates technology to help
students become 21st-century consumers and producers of information.

Johnston, Melissa P. 2012. "Connecting Teacher Librarians for Technology Integration Leadership." *School Libraries Worldwide* 18, no. 1:
18–33.
    Johnston identifies enablers and barriers for the librarian working to
integrate technology into teaching and learning.

Levitov, Deborah D. 2010. "The Need for Information Specialists." *School Library Monthly* 26, no. 7: 4.

Levitov suggests that librarians provide the space and the content for students to think and challenge ideas.

Levitov, Deborah D. 2012. "Authority as Information Specialists." *School Library Monthly* 28, no. 7: 4.

Levitov discusses the important role of the librarian in providing access to quality information.

Neuman, Delia. 2011. "Library Media Specialists: Premier Information Specialists for the Information Age." *TechTrends: Linking Research and Practice to Improve Learning* 55, no. 4: 21–26.

Neuman explains the librarian's various duties as an information specialist for students, teachers, and administrators.

REFERENCES

ABC-CLIO. 2015. *Explore. Connect. Understand.* Accessed June 13, 2015. https://www.ebscohost.com/us-high-schools/abc-clio

Alabama Virtual Library: Connecting You to a World of Knowledge. About the AVL Databases. n.d. Accessed June 13, 2015. http://www.avl.lib.al.us/nonauth/about/databases.php

All About Explorers. 2015. Accessed June 13, 2015. http://www.allaboutexplorers.com

California's Velcro Crop Under Challenge. 1996. Accessed June 13, 2015. https://web.archive.org/web/20071006093711/http://home.inreach.com/kumbach/velcro.html

Colonie Central High School. 2015. *CCHS Research Center.* Accessed June 14, 2015. http://www.livebinders.com/play/play?id=1603596

Creekview High School. 2015. *Welcome to LibGuides.* Accessed June 14, 2015. http://creekview.libguides.com/index.php

DigitalCitizenship.net. 2015. *Digital Citizenship: Using Technology Appropriately.* Accessed June 14, 2015. http://www.digitalcitizenship.net

FactMonster.com. 2015. Accessed June 13, 2015. http://www.factmonster.com/

Global Digital Citizen Foundation. 2015. *Digital Citizenship School Program.* Accessed June 14, 2015. http://globaldigitalcitizen.org/digital-citizenship-school-program

Halton County School Board. n.d. *Library Services: Elementary Pathfinders.* Accessed June 14, 2015. http://www.hdsb.ca/library/pages/elementarypathfinders.html

International Society for Technology in Education. 2007. *ISTE Standards: Students.* Accessed June 14, 2015. https://www.iste.org/docs/pdfs/20-14_ISTE_Standards-S_PDF.pdf

KidRex.org: Safe Search for Kids, by Kids. 2015. Accessed June 13, 2015. http://kidrex.org

KidsClick.org. 2011. Accessed June 13, 2015. http://kidsclick.org/

Lance, Keith Curry, Marcia J. Rodney, and Bill Schwarz. 2010. *The Idaho School Library Impact Study-2009: How Idaho Librarians, Teachers, and Administrators Collaborate for Student Success. Executive Summary.* Idaho Commission for Libraries. Accessed June 14, 2015. http://libraries.idaho.gov/files/Exec%20Sum%20Final.pdf

Lewis and Clark Elementary School. 2015. *Grade Level Links and Pathfinders.* Accessed June 14, 2015. https://lc-lps-ca.schoolloop.com/gllinks

NoodleTools. n.d. Smart Tools. Smart Research. Accessed June 14, 2015. http://www.noodletools.com/index.php

Online Dictionary of Library and Information Science (ODLIS). 2014. "Pathfinder." Accessed June 13, 2015. http://www.abc-clio.com/ODLIS/odlis_p.aspx

Pacific Northwest Tree Octopus. 2015. Accessed June 13, 2015. http://zapatopi.net/treeoctopus/

Purdue Online Writing Lab. 2015. Research and Citation Resources. Accessed June 14, 2015. https://owl.english.purdue.edu/owl/section/2/

Schrock, Kathy. 2015. 5 W's of Web Site Evaluation. Accessed June 13, 2015. http://www.schrockguide.net/uploads/3/9/2/2/392267/5ws.pdf

Schrock, Kathy. n.d. Research and Style Manual: Works Cited for Grades 1-6. Accessed June 14, 2015. http://www.schrockguide.net/uploads/3/9/2/2/392267/workscited_1_6.pdf

Smith, Ester. 2006. Student Learning Through Wisconsin School Library Media Centers: Case Study Report. Madison, WI: Wisconsin Department of Public Instruction, 2006. Wisconsin Department of Public Instruction. Accessed June 14, 2015. http://imt.dpi.wi.gov/files/imt/pdf/finalcasestudy.pdf

Thomas Dale High School. 2015. Pathfinders 9G. Accessed June 14, 2015. http://libguides.ccpsnet.net/tdhs/west/pathfinders

Todd, Ross J. and Carol C. Kuhlthau. 2004. Student Learning through Ohio School Libraries. Accessed July 8, 2015. http://webfiles.rbe.sk.ca/rps/terrance.pon/OELMAReportofFindings.pdf

The University of Chicago Laboratory Schools. 2015. Middle School Library Pathfinders. Accessed June 14, 2015. http://www.livebinders.com/play/play?id=1603596

Wyoming State Library. 2015. GoWYLD.net: Wyoming's Portal to Knowledge and Learning. Accessed June 13, 2015. http://gowyld.net/kids.html

4

LIBRARIAN AS INSTRUCTIONAL LEADER

"Librarians/media specialists are instrumental in enhancing teaching and learning in schools. Now more than ever they are shifting the culture of learning to prepare students for tomorrow's workforce through inquiry, exploration, problem solving, and collaboration."

Beth Niedermeyer, Ph.D., Superintendent, Noblesville Schools Educational Services Center, IN

Principals may not traditionally think of their school librarians as leaders within the school. Certainly if we think of the old-school librarian who maintained the library collection and felt that inventory was more important than student learning, leader is not the image or term that comes to mind. However, today's school librarian recognizes the key role that she plays in student learning and the potential impact that her instructional leadership within the school will provide.

While some librarians are "take-charge, full-speed-ahead" leaders, for the most part, librarians are leaders-from-the-middle. They model professional dispositions of concern, caring, persistence, and resiliency (Bush and Jones 2010). What does leading from the middle mean? Leading from the middle typically suggests not wanting or needing the spotlight but rather focusing on what is good for the overall mission of the school. Librarians, as leaders from the middle, will lead by example; they will take responsibility, question, and be able to answer why; and they will lead with energy, enthusiasm, and commitment (Shnall 2013).

CONNECTION TO SCHOOL MISSION AND STRATEGIC PLAN

Working with an overarching mission of student learning, it is simple to connect the mission of the library to the mission and strategic plan of the school. According to *Empowering Learners: Guidelines for School Library Programs*, "The mission of the school library program is to ensure that students and staff are effective users of ideas and information. The school librarian empowers students to be critical thinkers, enthusiastic readers, skillful researchers, and ethical users of information" (AASL 2009, 8).

Consider how closely the charge of the librarian—to empower students to be critical thinkers, enthusiastic readers, skillful researchers, and ethical users of information—aligns with the mission and strategic plan of 21st-century schools. Let's explore some examples:

- Mission Statement: Discovery Elementary School, Ashburn, Virginia, Loudoun County Public Schools: "Our mission as a Professional Learning Community is to ensure that EACH child who enters our school acquires the knowledge and skills that they need to achieve their full potential. . . . We do this so that they are uniquely prepared to meet the demands and challenges of our global society" (Discovery Elementary 2013, 3).
- Mission Statement: Carver Middle School, Chester, Virginia, Chesterfield County Public Schools: "Our mission is to help each student develop to his or her full potential. To this end, our staff provides a challenging environment in which students are expected to strive toward, meet, or surpass standards of academic performance" (Carver Middle 2014).
- Mission Statement: Marquette High School, Chesterfield, Missouri, Rockwood School District: "The mission of Marquette High School, home of the Mustangs, is to provide a safe and secure environment that will inspire, challenge, and encourage each student to develop a mature intellectual, creative, social, and physical foundation for lifelong learning in a global society . . . (Marquette High School n.d.).

As librarians work to help students become better readers, thinkers, and researchers, they lay a foundation for lifelong learning, inspiring and challenging each child to develop to full potential and imparting skills that enable future contributions to a global society.

Just as the alignment exists between the school and librarian missions, so does the connection between the librarian's mission and the school's strategic plan. As a team player and an instructional leader in the school, the librarian works to address key components of the school's strategic plan or, in many cases, school improvement plan.

If the school improvement plan identifies the need to increase reading test scores by 10 percent and diagnoses areas of greatest need to be (a) vocabulary and (b) main idea/supporting details, the librarian targets instruction in the library in these areas. If the school strategic plan calls for greater involvement with the local community, the librarian plans library events which bring community members into the school— author events, literacy nights, multicultural fairs—and which take the library out into the community—bookstore book fairs, mobile summer reading programs such as books on bikes.

PRINCIPAL'S ADVISORY COUNCIL

In order to work effectively toward addressing the school's improvement plan goals or strategic initiatives, the librarian must be fully involved in school initiatives. She should be a member of the principal's advisory council, school improvement committee, principal's leadership team—whatever name is given to the group of individuals who work with the principal to guide the direction of the school.

The librarian brings to this group knowledge of all areas of the curriculum, all grade levels, and all teachers in the school, knowledge which allows her to view issues through a larger lens. She should have access to all data that are utilized to drive the decision-making process, particularly student instructional performance data. As initiatives and options are discussed, in addition to noting how the library can support them, she can contribute the whole-school picture.

CURRICULUM DEVELOPMENT

As a teacher and instructional partner working with all grades and all content areas, the librarian has full knowledge of content area standards addressed in the school, *Common Core State Standards*, or state-specific curriculum standards. Because she has this cross-grade, cross-content knowledge, she can take a leadership role in the area of curriculum development.

Trained as a teacher, she understands content scope and sequence, developmentally appropriate instructional activities, and solid pedagogical practice. She knows what resources are available both online and within the library collection as well as additional resources that may be available for purchase. She identifies opportunities to improve student learning experiences with the incorporation of information literacy skills instruction. It is critical that she take a leadership role on curriculum development teams.

READING PROMOTER

A natural and expected leadership role for the school librarian is that of reading promoter. Reading promotion in a 21st-century library, however, goes beyond traditional readers' advisory services, helping children find "just the right book," and book checkout. Librarians provide book talks to encourage students to explore new authors and new genres as well as to share the newest and best books. They create book trailers to attract students to particular titles. They use QR codes to link author Web sites and online reviews to books in the collection. Knowing that students like to read books recommended by their peers, they load student-created book review podcasts in the online catalog or post them on the library Web page.

Librarians schedule author events in their schools; depending on the library budget, authors such as Henry Cole, Sharon Draper, Meg Medina, or Ben Mikaelsen might visit in person or they might visit via Skype. To encourage reading, librarians coordinate book competitions such as Battle of the Books, Virginia Readers' Choice, or, in Missouri, the Show Me Award, the Mark Twain Award, the Truman Readers Award, and the Gateway Readers Award. They may initiate a One Book, One

School program which allows everyone within the school community to have a shared reading experience.

LITERACY TEAM

As instructional leaders within the school, librarians not only promote reading but also have a place on the school literacy team. Librarians work with reading specialists, literacy coaches, and classroom teachers to plan and coordinate literacy experiences across the curriculum. Literacy, of course, includes not only reading and writing but also speaking, viewing, and listening, and the librarian, with her information specialist background and her whole-school view, can identify opportunities to incorporate multiple literacies into everything from daily lessons to whole-school events.

At the elementary level, activities might range from book buddy clubs to readers' theater presentations; at the middle school level, the literacy focus might be student-created public service announcements for the morning school news show; at the high school level oral history and digital records of community artifacts might be the focus. Whatever literacy initiative might be attempted, the librarian plays a valuable leadership role on the literacy team.

TECHNOLOGY INTEGRATION

Librarians are leaders in technology integration. From the days of filmstrips and transparencies to today's Web 2.0 tools, librarians have embraced current and emerging technologies, worked to master them, and then modeled their effective use. Librarians work with hardware—from iPads and Chromebooks to Promethean boards. Additionally, they work with presentation tools from PowerPoint and Prezi to Haiku Deck (a simple tool to create image-rich presentations on the Web or an iPad) and PowToon (where users can create animated videos and presentations).

They work with instructional content software such as Biblionasium (a reading community where children create, share, and retrieve book recommendations) and Figment (a shared writing community), Historypin (a global community where users can share and post historical content) and Vocabulary.com (an interactive vocabulary game and dictionary), and Wonderopolis (a site for curiosity and exploration). They keep current on instructional technological tools and take a leadership role in their integration and implementation in both the library and classrooms.

PROFESSIONAL DEVELOPMENT PROVIDER

Librarians are in-house, resident providers of professional development for faculty and staff. An example of one area in which they can provide professional development is the use of Web 2.0 tools. Carl Harvey, librarian at North Elementary School (Indiana), indicates that, at his principal's request, he led his entire staff through their yearlong professional development with staff meetings that focused on one tool at a time, grade-level PLC meetings to practice, and assistance as needed for effective implementation in the classroom (Harvey 2013, 33).

Using a similar format, librarians can introduce their teachers to subscription databases. School districts make a significant financial investment in online subscription databases, from Capstone's *PebbleGo* for early elementary grades to Gale's *National Geographic Kids* for middle grades to Gale's *Contemporary Literary Criticism* for upper-level English classes. Librarians can lead grade-level, content-specific, hands-on workshops for faculty to increase both awareness of instructional possibilities and comfort level in using.

For example, in a focus on 21st-century skills in their *Design for Excellence 2020 School Improvement Plan for 2013-2014 School Year*, Meadowbrook High School, Chesterfield County (Virginia), included the following as an action step: "On the early release professional development days, teachers will collaborate utilizing blended learning module resources to enhance 21st century skills. While completing the modules, PLCs will begin to brainstorm ways to enhance collaboration, communication, critical thinking, and problem solving using resources such as Edmodo, Google Docs, Discovery Education, Mackin Via and library databases" (3). Through targeted teacher training sessions, librarians can facilitate the use of the resources.

Another area in which librarians can provide much-needed professional development for their faculty members is copyright and intellectual property. Just as librarians teach students to respect the intellectual property of others, to paraphrase, and to cite sources, they can share information with their colleagues as well. A workshop on what educational fair use of copyrighted material truly allows provides critical information for teachers. Hands-on exploration of the creative commons and its tremendous wealth of resources raises awareness of the copyright-friendly material available there and the options for sharing intellectual property.

MODEL FOR PROFESSIONAL GROWTH

Librarians serve as instructional leaders in their schools also as they model continued professional growth. Whereas classroom teachers typically work as grade levels, on teams, or as departments, most school librarians work solo. Knowing that their profession is in an ongoing state of change and growth, they realize that continued professional development is critical to remaining current in the field.

Librarians model continued professional growth for teacher colleagues as they attend library, technology, and reading conferences and as they participate in relevant webinars. They take advantage of librarian online communities of practice. They subscribe to library Listservs and follow library leaders' blogs. They participate in Connected Educator Month, they explore Pinterest for anything library related, and they meet and share on Twitter. As they constantly strive to fine-tune their knowledge and skills, they not only model lifelong learning for their colleagues but also, in their leadership role within the school, implement what they have learned.

BEYOND SCHOOL WALLS TO COMMUNITY

If the library is the heart and hub of the school and the librarian serves as an instructional leader, a key task as instructional leader is that of representing the school and library to the larger learning community. It is critical that members of the school community understand that to-

day's school library is not merely a collection of books and other resources but rather a place of active learning.

As an instructional leader, the librarian makes connections with parents and other community leaders and with the local public library. To
bring parents and other stakeholders into the library, she hosts literacy
fairs, speaks at parent-teacher association meetings, sponsors mother-
daughter/father-son book clubs, and participates in community-
sponsored author events. For example, as part of the 2013 All Henrico
Reads, when *New York Times* best-selling author Adriana Trigiani visit-
ed Glen Allen High School, Henrico County (Virginia) Public Schools
(Moomaw n.d.), the school librarians were actively involved in the
event.

As instructional leaders, school librarians work to build community
support for their library programs. Connection with the community is
vital as evidenced by the following statement on the Swan Valley High
School Library Media Center, Saginaw, Michigan, Web site. Swan Valley High was named the 2013 AASL School Library Program of the
Year.

> PARTNERSHIPS: Our library program thrives because of the sup-
> port of our students, staff, parents and community. With the leader-
> ship provided by MAME (Michigan Association for Media in Educa-
> tion), the American Library Association and American Association of
> School Librarians, and support from the Library of Michigan and
> Michigan eLibrary, the Michigan Humanities Council, National
> Endowment for the Arts, the Saginaw Arts & Enrichment Commis-
> sion, the Michigan Council for Arts & Cultural Affairs, United Way
> (Volunteer START), the Saginaw Community Foundation, Nexteer,
> Meijer, HSC, and many other local businesses, individuals, and com-
> munity groups, we are able to meet the needs of our patrons. We are
> continually grateful to all of these individuals and groups for their
> continued support and guidance (Swan Valley n.d.).

RESEARCH FINDINGS ON THE IMPACT OF THE LIBRARIAN AS INSTRUCTIONAL LEADER

- According to *How School Librarians Help Kids Achieve Standards:
  The Second Colorado Study* (Lance, Rodney, and Hamilton-Pennell

2000), "test scores increase as library media specialists spend more time providing in-service training to teachers" (4).

- According to *How Students, Teachers & Principals Benefit from Strong School Libraries: The Indiana Study* (RSL Research 2007), "across grade levels, better performing schools also tended to be those whose principals valued . . . having their LMSs serve on key school committees" (1). In fact, "almost all responding principals reported considering it essential or desirable that . . . the LMS be appointed to key school committees (96%), and the LMS provide in-service opportunities to faculty (97%)" (67).
- According to *Measuring Up to Standards: The Impact of School Library Programs and Information Literacy in Pennsylvania Schools* (Lance, Rodney, and Hamilton-Pennell 2000), "Test scores increase as school librarians spend more time . . . providing in-service training to teachers; serving on standards committee[s]; serving on curriculum committee[s] (7)."
- According to the New York Comprehensive Center's *Informational Brief: Impact of School Libraries on Student Achievement* (2011), "school librarian involvement in professional development activities creates a school environment that promotes leadership and achievement" (12).

IN SUMMARY: LIBRARIAN AS INSTRUCTIONAL LEADER

In order to maximize contributions to the school, the librarian should serve as an instructional leader. She should connect the library program to the school's mission and strategic plan, serve on the principal's advisory council, participate actively in curriculum development, promote reading, serve on the literacy team, foster the integration of technology into instruction, provide professional development for faculty members, model professional growth, and connect the library to the larger school community. Research findings demonstrate that librarian leadership activities such as these contribute positively to student learning.

ADDITIONAL READINGS

Achterman, Doug. 2010. "21st-Century Literacy Leadership." *School Library Monthly* 26, no. 10: 41–43.

Achterman offers information about literacy leadership, the cornerstone of lifelong learning at the core of a school library program's mission.

Devaney, Laura. 2013. "School Librarians Are Rising School Leaders." *Eschool News* 16, no. 10: 25.

Devaney reveals that U.S. school librarians are shaking off the old stereotype that they are isolated from a school's teachers, students, and classrooms.

Everhart, Nancy. 2007. "Leadership: School Library Media Specialists as Effective School Leaders." *Knowledge Quest* 35, no. 4: 54–57.

Everhart discusses how school librarians become effective school leaders who make greater opportunities for learners, serving as the technology leader in the school by giving staff development and modeling ethical and important application of technology.

Green, Lucy Santos. 2014. "Through the Looking Glass." *Knowledge Quest* 43, no. 1: 36–43.

Green discusses the role of school librarians as leaders who make meaningful contributions toward the integration of technology and learning.

Johnston, Melissa P. 2013. "Taking the Lead with Technology Integration." *School Library Monthly* 29, no. 4: 33–35.

Johnston focuses on the leadership role of school librarians related to technology integration and emphasizes the role of school librarians in preparing students for the future and developing information skills to allow them to use technology in learning.

Johnston, Melissa P. 2012. "Connecting Teacher Librarians for Technology Integration Leadership." *School Libraries Worldwide* 18, no. 1: 18–33.

Teacher-librarians have a vital role to play in making certain that students develop the 21st-century skills that will enable them to use technology as a tool for learning and to participate in a digital culture.

King, Alanna. 2012. "Redefining Reading and the Role of the Teacher-Librarian." *School Libraries in Canada (17108535)* 30, no. 3: 25–29.

King focuses on teaching reading online and the role of teacher-librarian. Topics discussed include the four interrelated factors that have changed the nature of literacy, reading in multiple dimensions, and the challenge for the school librarian as a literacy leader.

Starkey, Carolyn. 2012. "Releasing Your Inner Leader." *Knowledge Quest* 40, no. 3: 10–13.

Starkey focuses on school librarians' role in enhancing teacher effectiveness, improving student achievement, and providing leadership to transform their school community into a true collaborative culture.

REFERENCES

American Association of School Librarians. 2009. *Empowering Learners: Guidelines for School Library Programs*. Chicago, IL: American Library Association.

Bush, Gail, and Jami B. Jones. 2010. *Tales Out of the School Library: Developing Professional Dispositions*. Santa Barbara, CA: Libraries Unlimited.

Carver Middle School: About Us. 2014. Accessed November 28, 2014. http://www.carver. mychesterfieldschools.com/pages/Carver_Middle/School_Information/Page_Menu/ About_Us

Design for Excellence: Meadowbrook High School School Improvement Plan for 2013-2014. n.d. Accessed November 28, 2014. http://www.meadowbrookhs.mychesterfieldschools. com/files/_yHJFr_/9cd151a5e3241cdc3745a49013852ec4/Meadowbrook_HS_Webpage_ for_SIP_Design_for_Excellence_2020.pdf

Discovery Elementary School Parent-Student Handbook. 2013. Accessed November 28, 2014. http://www.lcps.org/cms/lib4/VA01000195/Centricity/Domain/15139/ HANDBOOK_Discovery_2013-2014.pdf

Harvey, Carl A. 2013. "Putting on the Professional Development Hat." *School Library Monthly* 29, no. 5: 32–34.

Lance, Keith Curry, Marcia J. Rodney, and Christine Hamilton-Pennell. 2000. *How School Librarians Help Kids Achieve Standards: The Second Colorado Study*. Denver, CO: Colorado State Library, Colorado Department of Education. Accessed November 28, 2014. http://www.lrs.org/documents/lmcstudies/CO/execsumm.pdf

Lance, Keith Curry, Marcia J. Rodney, and Christine Hamilton-Pennell. 2000. *Measuring Up to Standards: The Impact of School Library Programs and Information Literacy in Pennsylvania Schools*. Greensburg, PA: Pennsylvania Citizens for Better Libraries. Accessed November 28, 2014. http://files.eric.ed.gov/fulltext/ED446771.pdf

Marquette High School: About Us: Mission Statement. n.d. Accessed November 28, 2014. http://www.rockwood.k12.mo.us/marquette/aboutus/Pages/default.aspx

Moomaw, Graham. n.d. "Novelist Trigiani Offers Advice to Henrico Students." Accessed November 28, 2014. http://www.timesdispatch.com/news/local/henrico/novelist-trigiani-offers-advice-to-henrico-students/article_77db2115-bab7-53ad-b6c2-2895371284b6. html?mode=jqm

New York Comprehensive Center. 2011, October. *Informational Brief: Impact of School Libraries on Student Achievement*. Accessed November 28, 2014. http://www.nysl.nysed. gov/libdev/nyla/nycc_school_library_brief.pdf

RSL Research. 2007. *How Students, Teachers & Principals Benefit from Strong School Libraries: The Indiana Study*. Accessed November 28, 2014. http://c.ymcdn.com/sites/www.ilfonline.org/resource/resmgr/aisle/infinalreportnextsteps.pdf

Shnall, Tal. 2013, October 6. "Four Ways to Lead from the Middle." Accessed November 28, 2014. http://leadershipcafe.org/2013/10/06/four-ways-to-lead-from-the-middle/

Swan Valley High School: Swan Valley High School Library Media Center. n.d. Accessed November 28, 2014. http://swanvalleyschools.com/highschool/teachers/kay-wejrowski/

5

LIBRARIAN AS PROGRAM ADMINISTRATOR

"The library is the hub of the building. A dead library = a dead learning environment. The librarian is a master curriculum designer who cultivates a love for learning through reading. This love leaves students empowered, inspired, and educated so that they reach their full potential as lifelong learners in a diverse world."

B. Michelle Maultsby-Springer, Ed.D., Executive Principal, Croft Middle Design Center, Metropolitan Nashville Public Schools, TN

In his classic work, *Taxonomies of the School Library Media Program*, David Loertscher suggests that the basic level for a school library program is that of a "smoothly operating information infrastructure" (18). This foundation must be in place with all components working together in order for the program to function efficiently and effectively and to make full contributions to the broader instructional program of the school and to student learning.

Various components of the school library program fit together like interlocking pieces of a puzzle: developing the collection to support curriculum and instruction, supporting intellectual freedom, providing access to both physical and virtual resources, coordinating staffing for a unified program of services to students and teachers, creating a positive library environment which fosters learning, and utilizing data and evidence to formulate a strategic plan that moves the library forward in alignment with the school's mission and goals. As program administrator, the librarian coordinates these activities, typically as an invisible, behind-the-scenes part of her job.

COLLECTION TO SUPPORT CURRICULUM AND INSTRUCTION

The librarian is tasked with building a collection of resources that supports the instructional and informational needs of students and teachers. The collection will include print books, nonprint materials such as videos, and digital, and electronic resources such as databases and e-books. To choose materials to add to the library collection, the librarian follows selection criteria as set forth in district policy.

As the librarian evaluates materials for potential purchase, she uses criteria such as content, scope of the work, accuracy of information presented in the work, authority of the author/creator, currency of information, absence of bias, age and grade-level appropriateness, and, of course, cost. In order to spend funds as wisely as possible, she uses professional selection tools (such as *Best Books for Children*, Libraries Unlimited, 2015) for recommendations, and she reads professional reviews of materials (such as those in *School Library Connection*). Selection of materials is deliberate, as the librarian works to build resources to support the school's instructional, information, and recreational reading needs.

Since funds are never unlimited in a school setting, the librarian constantly makes choices. Which area of the library collection is most in need of updating? As collaborative lessons are completed, which areas of the collection do teachers say need additional resources or resources on a different reading level or in a different format? The librarian has ongoing "wish lists" or consideration files of materials that are needed. Should extra funds be available, for example at the end of the school year, the librarian can be counted on to spend them wisely to enhance the library collection.

INTELLECTUAL FREEDOM

As a program administrator who builds and provides access to the library collection, a school librarian stands for intellectual freedom and access to information. According to the American Association of School Librarians' *Access to Resources and Services in the School Library Media Program: An Interpretation of the Library Bill of Rights* (2014), "school librarians resist efforts by individuals or groups to define what is appropriate for all students or teachers to read, view, hear, or access regardless of technology, formats or method of delivery."

As the librarian builds the collection, she provides materials that represent diverse points of view. The library is a place where students ask questions and seek information, think critically, and learn to formulate their own conclusions. The student writing a paper on climate change or the death penalty must have access to information on both sides of the issue in order to successfully complete his research. If materials are challenged, the librarian follows district policy for their review and reconsideration.

ACCESS

As program administrator, the librarian works to ensure that students and teachers have both physical and virtual access to information. Thinking of physical access, shelving needs to be at the appropriate height for grade levels in the school, and aisles and furniture need to be wheelchair-accessible. Areas of the library should be clearly marked with easily read signage. If color is used, an alternate presentation of information, for example text, should also be provided to accommodate students with color vision deficiencies. The librarian should implement the principles of universal design.

The library should be open and available for student and teacher use—before, during, and after the school day. If feasible, the library may be open one evening a month for family literacy nights. During the summer it may be open one morning a week to allow students continued access to books over the summer months. Throughout the year policies regarding checkout of materials should promote rather than hinder usage. The purpose of the library is to provide access to information. Policies which unnecessarily restrict the number of books or the assigned reading level of the book a student can check out should be considered carefully.

Libraries function best and contribute most to student learning when they are flexibly scheduled. A flexibly scheduled library allows access at the point of instructional need. According the *Position Statement on Flexible Scheduling* from the American Association of School Librarians (2014),

> the integrated library program philosophy requires an open schedule that includes flexible and equitable access to physical and virtual collections for staff and students. Classes must be flexibly scheduled into the library on an as needed basis to facilitate just-in-time research, training, and utilization of technology with the guidance of the teacher who is the subject specialist, and the librarian who is the information process specialist. The resulting lesson plans recognize that the length of the learning experience is dependent on learning needs rather than a fixed library time.

Thinking of virtual access, e-book and database subscriptions are wasted if students are unaware that they exist or are unable to access them. Access may be provided through the school's online catalog, the library Web page, or class or library pages in the school's learning management system (such as Blackboard or Canvas).

Students must know where to locate virtual resources, and they must know the required log-in ID and password if accessing from outside of the school. Log-ins and passwords can be provided in student handbooks or agenda books, on bookmarks, or on library handouts. Due to licensing agreements with the vendors, log-in and password information should not be publicly available on the Web. As program administrator, the librarian works to ensure physical and virtual access to resources.

STAFFING

As noted previously, "the mission of the school library program is to ensure that students and staff are effective users of ideas and information. The school librarian empowers students to be critical thinkers, enthusiastic readers, skillful researchers, and ethical users of information" (AASL 2009, 8). To accomplish these goals, the school librarian must be a teacher and instructional partner. The majority of her time should be focused on instructional tasks, collaboration, and teaching.

Much work, however, goes into a smoothly functioning library program. Support staff to provide clerical assistance is critical. Job titles vary from state to state and school district to school district, but this person—assistant, clerk, paraprofessional, secretary—is key to implementing the library's mission. Parent volunteers can also provide assistance for the librarian by helping with book fairs, assisting with events such as family literacy nights, or simply shelving books. Student workers can be trained and utilized from upper elementary through senior high. These students gain valuable experience and typically take ownership of the library program.

The librarian is trained as a teacher who has further specialized in school librarianship coursework. The best utilization of her time and skill set is on activities that directly impact student learning. Additional staffing—either paid or volunteer—in the library allows for the most productive use of the librarian's time. As program administrator, she delegates duties as appropriate.

LIBRARY ENVIRONMENT

The library is the largest instructional space within the school. The librarian works to create not only an attractive, warm, and inviting physical space but also a culture of welcome and acceptance. It is a space for reading, inquiry, and learning, and it is a space where collaboration occurs. Collaboration can take the form of the teacher and librarian co-planning, co-teaching, and co-evaluating lessons, or it can take the form of students working together on research and projects.

"The libraries of the 21st century provide a welcoming common space that encourages exploration, creation, and collaboration between students, teachers, and a broader community. They bring together the best of the physical and digital to create learning hubs" (Holland 2015). The 21st-century library is a learning commons where students actively participate in their learning and think, create, share, and grow (AASL 2015).

Many school libraries now have makerspaces, spaces in the library in which students "make" something in hands-on learning. Depending on grade level and availability of resources, making comes in a limitless variety of forms: from writing poetry, recording music, knitting, or crocheting to making bookmarks, building with Legos, or working with electronic circuits. Making can be simple or it can be complex, addressing various STEM challenges. It allows for critical thinking, problem solving, and collaborative group work.

The library environment begins in the physical space of the library itself, but it encompasses much more. It extends beyond the four walls to a mindset and culture of learning. Through resources, services, and activities, the library program is the instructional and intellectual hub of the school. As program administrator, the librarian cultivates the environment that fosters this mindset.

ATTENTION TO DATA

Librarians pay close attention to data. Collection statistics are important: as program administrator, the librarian monitors the age of the collection, weeding outdated and inaccurate resources. If science is a curriculum emphasis, she pays careful attention to the nonfiction 500s Science section to be sure that an adequate quantity of resources are available. If the school's curriculum focus is on languages, she targets the nonfiction 400s Language section. An emphasis on performing arts requires close scrutiny of the 700s Arts and Recreation.

Circulation statistics are important. The librarian monitors them to see which areas of the collection should be enhanced. If graphic novels fly off the shelves, more graphic novel titles should be purchased. If biographies are the items in demand, additional ones should be added to the collection. The librarian also monitors usage statistics: which grade levels or departments use the library most? Which teachers collaborate most often? She will use this data, not only to include in the library end-of-the-year report but also to target future collaborative efforts.

Student data are critically important. The librarian will document how she makes a difference in student learning. Is there a correlation between student book checkout and student reading scores? Do students in classes where the librarian collaboratively taught information literacy skills score higher on standardized tests than students in classes where no collaboration has occurred? As program administrator, the librarian monitors and shares this data.

EVIDENCE-BASED PRACTICE

As the administrator of a 21st-century school library program, the school librarian embraces evidence-based practice. "Evidence-based school librarianship uses research-derived evidence to shape and direct what we do. EBP combines professional wisdom, reflective experience, and understanding of students' needs with the judicious use of re-search-derived evidence to make decisions about how the school library can best meet the instructional goals of the school" (Todd 2008).

According to Todd (2009, 89), the librarian utilizes evidence for practice, evidence in practice, and evidence of practice. She uses re-search evidence to implement best practice in the library program, then collects and shares the results. For example, a recent study conducted by Loertscher (2014) found "when teachers teach alone in classrooms, about 50% of the students were likely to meet or exceed that teacher's highest expectations. When coteaching occurred, 70-100% of the students were likely to meet or exceed the pair's expectations using normal assessment measures" (13).

Using the results of this study (evidence for practice), the librarian co-teaches a research unit on nutrition with the health teacher (evidence in practice). At the conclusion of the research unit, she collects data from students and the collaborating teacher on the difference her participation made in student learning and shares this data with faculty members and school administrators (evidence of practice).

STRATEGIC PLAN

As program administrator, the librarian, with input from stakeholders (students, teachers, administrators, parents, and community members) develops a strategic plan for the library program. The goals and objectives set forth in this strategic plan align with and support the mission, goals, and objectives of the school. Operational decisions for the library program then are based on this strategic plan.

RESEARCH FINDINGS ON THE IMPACT OF THE LIBRARIAN AS PROGRAM ADMINISTRATOR

- According to *The Impact of New York's School Libraries on Student Achievement and Motivation: Phase III* (Small, Shanahan, and Stasak 2010), "elementary students in schools with certified school librarians are more likely to have higher English and language arts (ELA) scores than those in schools with noncertified school librarians" (2).
- According to *How Pennsylvania School Libraries Pay Off: Investment in Student Achievement and Academic Standards. PA School Library Project* (Lance and Schwarz 2012), "on average, the percentage of students scoring Advanced in Writing is two and a half times higher for schools with vs. schools without a full-time, certified librarian (13.2% vs. 5.3%). Similarly, the average percentage of students scoring Advanced in Writing is almost twice as high for schools with a full-time, certified librarian with support staff vs. those with a full-time certified librarian alone (16.7% vs. 9.2%)" (v).
- According to *Check It Out! The Results of the School Library Media Census* (Baxter and Smalley 2004), "the larger the budget for books and electronic resources of a Minnesota elementary school media center, the higher a student's reading achievement. There is a statistically significant relationship between higher reading scores and larger school media center budgets at the elementary level" (15).
- According to *Haves, Halves, and Have-Nots: School Libraries and Student Achievement in California* (Achterman 2008), "at the high school level . . . there was a significant correlation between total budget and both English Language Arts and History CST scores" (185).
- According to *School Librarian Staffing Levels and Student Achievement as Represented in 2006–2009 Kansas Annual Yearly Progress Data* (Dow, Lakin, and Court 2012), "students in high poverty (33–67 percent free and reduced-price lunch) with a full-time school librarian achieve approximately 13 points higher in math than those with no school librarian" (12).

- According to *Powerful Libraries Make Powerful Learners: The Illinois Study* (Lance, Rodney, and Hamilton-Pennell 2005), "elementary schools with more flexibly scheduled libraries performed 10 percent better in reading and 11 percent better in writing on the ISAT tests of fifth-graders than schools with less flexibly scheduled libraries. Where high school libraries are more flexibly scheduled, more than six percent more eleventh-graders met or exceeded PSAE reading standards than their counterparts with less flexibly scheduled libraries. High schools with more flexibly scheduled libraries also had five percent higher ACT scores than schools with less flexibly scheduled libraries" (ii).
- According to *Haves, Halves, and Have-Nots: School Libraries and Student Achievement in California* (Achterman 2008), "In a declining economy, the number of hours a school library remains open can be critical, especially for students without access to books or technology at home. The California study draws attention to the importance of access to the school library and its resources in addressing educational equity" (Kachel 2013, 15).

IN SUMMARY: LIBRARIAN AS PROGRAM ADMINISTRATOR

When the librarian works as a program administrator, much of the work accomplished is behind the scenes. She develops a collection that supports the instructional program of the school, advocates for intellectual freedom, and works to provide access to both physical and virtual resources. She coordinates staffing and fosters the library learning environment. With attention to data and through evidence-based practice, she develops a strategic plan that connects the library to the instructional program of the school. Research findings demonstrate that effective library programs contribute to student learning.

ADDITIONAL READINGS

Adams, Helen R. 2015. "Have Intellectual Freedom and Privacy Questions? Help Is on the Way." *Knowledge Quest* 43, no. 4: 72–75.

Adams highlights key issues of intellectual freedom and privacy in school libraries as she looks forward to a new resource from the American Library Association.

Bentheim, Christina A. 2014. "Looking Back on a Year of Transition from Traditional Library to Learning Commons." *Teacher Librarian* 41, no. 5: 50–53.
Bentheim discusses the transition from traditional library to a library learning commons that aligns with the school's improvement plan.

Donnelly, Andria. 2015. "Making the Transition to a Collaborative Flexible Schedule." *School Library Monthly* 31, no. 7: 32–33.
Donnelly provides scheduling tips, lesson planning tips, and organization tips for those transitioning from a fixed to a flexible schedule.

Harvey II, Carl A. 2014/2015. "The Schedule Spectrum." *School Library Monthly* 31, no. 3:17–19.
Harvey defines "fixed," "flexible," and "hybrid" schedules and explores access to the collection, instruction, and facilities through the lens of each schedule type.

Hughes, Hilary. 2014. "School Libraries, Teacher-Librarians and Student Outcomes: Presenting and Using the Evidence." *School Libraries Worldwide* 20, no. 1: 29–50.
Hughes examines research in Australia and the United States regarding the impact of libraries and librarians on student learning and suggests how this evidence can be used to strengthen library programs.

Hyman, Shannon C. 2014. "Planning and Creating a Library Learning Commons." *Teacher Librarian* 41, no. 3: 16–21.
Hyman shares her story of opening a new elementary school library learning commons where the focus is inquiry, engagement, and creativity.

Martin, Ann M. 2011. "Data-Driven Leadership." *School Library Monthly* 28, no. 2: 31–33.
Martin gives the rationale, then outlines the steps for collecting, organizing, and sharing data to demonstrate evidence and justify needs to assist in program growth.

Moorefield-Lang, Heather. 2015. "Change in the Making: Makerspaces and the Ever-Changing Landscape of Libraries." *TechTrends: Linking Research and Practice to Improve Learning* 59, no. 3: 107–12.

The author shares her findings from a recent study regarding the implementation of makerspaces in libraries.

Velasco, Moses. 2014. "Positive Climates for Learning." *Teaching Librarian* 22, no. 1: 25–27.

Velasco discusses designing the library to stimulate learning, exploring the connection between the learning commons and positive school climates.

Yates, Steven D. 2011. "The School Librarian as Program Administrator: Just-In-Time Librarianship." *Knowledge Quest* 39, no. 5, 42–44.

Yates provides an overview of advocacy, library collections, and other facets of library program administration.

REFERENCES

Achterman, Douglas L. 2008. "Haves, Halves, and Have-Nots: School Libraries and Student Achievement in California." Diss. University of North Texas, UNT Digital Library. Accessed June 22, 2015. http://digital.library.unt.edu/ark:/67531/metadc9800/

American Association of School Librarians. 2009. *Empowering Learners: Guidelines for School Library Programs.* Chicago: American Library Association.

American Association of School Librarians. 2014. "Access to Resources and Services in the School Library Media Program: An Interpretation of the Library Bill of Rights." Accessed June 22, 2015. http://www.ala.org/advocacy/intfreedom/librarybill/interpretations/accessresources

American Association of School Librarians. 2014. "Position Statement on Flexible Scheduling." Accessed June 22, 2015. http://www.ala.org/aasl/advocacy/resources/statements/flexsched

American Association of School Librarians. 2015. "School Librarians and Learning4Life." Accessed July 4, 2015. http://www.ala.org/aasl/learning4life/school-librarians

Baxter, Susan J., and Ann Walker Smalley. 2004. "Check It Out! The Results of the School Library Media Census." St. Paul, MN: Metronet. Accessed June 22, 2015. http://www.metrolibraries.net/res/pdfs/2004final_report.pdf

Dow, Mirah J., Jacqueline McMahon Lakin, and Stephen C. Court. 2012. "School Librarian Staffing Levels and Student Achievement as Represented in 2006–2009 Kansas Annual Yearly Progress Data." *School Library Research* 15: 1–15. Accessed June 22, 2015. http://www.ala.org/aasl/sites/ala.org.aasl/files/content/aaslpubsandjournals/slr/vol15/SLR_StaffingLevelsandStudentAchievement_V15.pdf

Holland, Beth. 2015. "21st Century Libraries: The Learning Commons." Accessed July 4, 2015. http://www.edutopia.org/blog/21st-century-libraries-learning-commons-beth-holland

Kachel, Debra V. 2013. "School Library Research Summarized: A Graduate Class Project." Accessed June 22, 2015. http://sl-it.mansfield.edu/upload/MU-LibAdvoBklt2013.pdf

Lance, Keith Curry, Marcia J. Rodney, and Christine Hamilton-Pennell. 2005. "Powerful Libraries Make Powerful Learners: The Illinois Study." Canton, IL: Illinois School Library Media Association. Accessed June 22, 2015. http://www.islma.org/pdf/ILStudy2.pdf

Lance, Keith Curry, and Bill Schwarz. 2012. "How Pennsylvania School Libraries Pay Off: Investments in Student Achievement and Academic Standards. PA School Library Project. Executive Summary." Accessed June 22, 2015. http://lgdata.s3-website-us-east-1. amazonaws.com/docs/2788/580939/PAreport-execsummaryrenum.pdf

Loertscher, David V. 2000. *Taxonomies of the School Library Media Program.* 2nd ed. Jose, CA: HiWillow.

Loertscher, David V. 2014. "Collaboration and Coteaching: A New Measure of Impact." *Teacher Librarian* 42, no. 2: 8–19.

Small, Ruth V., Kathryn A. Shanahan, and Megan Stasak. 2010. "The Impact of New York's School Libraries on Student Achievement and Motivation: Phase III." *School Library Media Research* 13: 1–31 Accessed June 22, 2015. http://www.ala.org/aasl/sites/ala.org. aasl/files/content/aaslpubsandjournals/slr/vol13/SLR_ImpactofNewYork.pdf

Todd, Ross. 2008. "The Evidence-Based Manifesto for School Librarians." Accessed July 4, 2015. http://www.slj.com/2008/04/sljarchives/the-evidence-based-manifesto-for-school-librarians/#_

Todd, Ross J. 2009. "School Librarianship and Evidence Based Practice: Progress, Perspectives, and Challenges." *Evidence Based Library and Information Practice* 4, no. 2: 78–96.

6

CHALLENGES AND BENEFITS

School librarians of the 21st century are key instructional personnel in a school building. They function as teachers, instructional partners, information specialists, instructional leaders, and program administrators. Numerous research studies have demonstrated that when they take an active role in the instructional program of the school, student achievement is higher. What then are the challenges and the benefits of tapping into the skills of 21st-century school librarians?

CHALLENGES

Previous Perceptions

How do principals know what to expect of their school librarians? Through readings in professional journals? By attending conference sessions? From topics and discussions in principal preparation coursework? Not the case, it seems. Exploration of journals and textbooks used in educational administration courses reveals that school library topics are seldom included (Kaplan 2006, Veltze 1992).

Over 75 percent of NCATE-accredited graduate principal-preparation programs surveyed reported that they did not include information about school libraries and school librarians in their coursework (Wilson and McNeil 1998). Gary Hartzell suggests that

Most full time EdAd [educational administration] professors are former practitioners. In essence, each generation of school administrators is trained and prepared by the previous one. Principals and
superintendents who later become professors weren't taught the value of libraries in their own university training, and they didn't learn it
on the job. As a result, they don't integrate any sense of library value
into the courses they teach to aspiring principals and superintendents intent on earning their degrees and credentials (2012, 2).

Findings from numerous studies suggest that principals learn what
librarians do from librarians with whom they've worked in the past,
either as fellow classroom teachers (Church 2008, 2010; Hartzell 2002)
or as administrators (Alexander, Smith, and Carey 2003; Church 2008,
2010). It seems, therefore, that principals' perceptions of librarians are
based on personal experiences with librarians with whom they have
worked—which brings us to another issue.

Librarians of the 20th Century

Some of you reading this book have been nodding in agreement at the
description of the various activities and tasks of 21st-century school
librarians. You understand that librarians teach information literacy and
inquiry skills. You have seen your librarian collaborate with classroom
teachers and technology integrators to team teach a lesson. You know
that your librarian is well-versed in information resources, have observed her conducting a professional development workshop for teachers on a new technology tool, and see your library as a learning commons for your school. Others of you may have been shaking your head
in confusion or disbelief.

In their 2009 article, "Things That Keep Us Up at Night," Joyce
Kasman Valenza and Doug Johnson address this very topic. They share,

How do we reach, wake up, and retool the profession for changes
that need to be made today and impact us all? We need to prepare
young people for a highly connected world. Librarians who don't
have PLNs [professional learning networks], don't attend conferences, don't read cutting-edge professional literature—from both the
library and the education worlds—are dragging our profession down.
And good people are going with them (30).

Allison Bernstein expresses similar sentiments in her 2011 article, "The Big Elephant in the Library."

> As a profession we need to take an objective look at ourselves. Unfortunately, I think it is within our own ranks that we can find those individuals who do the most damage. Yes, I said it. It's the elephant in the room. It's us. Or should I say, not those of us who are reading and implementing the advice in this magazine, but our colleagues who continue the stereotype of the librarian who simply holds storytime each week during their library period, followed by a book checkout time, who teaches kids to use a resource in a vacuum, or—worse yet—who always shushes everyone (46).

Sadly, very sadly, 20th-century librarians still exist: librarians who consider the library a sacred and quiet place, who guard their books and restrict access to information, who teach traditional library lessons in standard lecture format but do not truly see themselves as teachers, who celebrate a robust, current, and well-rounded collection as the ultimate sign of a strong library program.

In contrast, school librarians of the 21st century understand the importance of being fully connected to the instructional program of the school and understand that they must work constantly to keep up in an ever-changing and growing profession. They know that the true measure of a successful library program is its impact on student learning.

Since you have now read this book, and you now know that your librarian should be a teacher, instructional partner, information specialist, instructional leader, and program administrator, you can set reasonable performance expectations. Many 20th-century librarians, realizing that you understand and appreciate what their job entails, will rise to the occasion and work toward implementing their various roles. Which brings us to yet another issue . . .

BUDGET AND STAFFING

Do you have a full-time, certified librarian within your school? *Empowering Learners: Guidelines for School Library Programs* (AASL 2009) states as a guideline in the "Building the Learning Environment" chapter: "The school library program has a minimum of one full-time certified/licensed school librarian supported by qualified staff sufficient for the school's instructional programs, services, facilities, size, and number of teachers and students" (29).

Some states require that each school have a full-time certified librarian. In Virginia, for example, school librarians are classified as instructional personnel, and staffing is mandated in the state's *Standards of Quality* as follows: "Librarians in elementary schools, one part-time to 299 students, one full-time at 300 students; librarians in middle schools, one-half time to 299 students, one full-time at 300 students, two full-time at 1,000 students; librarians in high schools, one half-time to 299 students, one full-time at 300 students, two full-time at 1,000 students" (Virginia Dept. of Ed. 2014).

Many states do not have this requirement in place, however. Staffing requirements vary greatly from state to state, and due to challenging economic times over the past decade, previous staffing mandates for library staffing have been relaxed. School librarian positions have been eliminated in many states.

"Sadly, there currently are only about 800 credentialed teacher librarians working in the entire state of California . . . (Compare that, for example, to the state of Texas, with a similar school population and about 4,600 credentialed librarians.) Moreover, approximately 20 percent of California's schools don't even have a functioning library, and, of the 80 percent that do, 80 percent are run by non-teaching staff" (Lofton 2015).

In Philadelphia, "in 1991, there were 176 certified librarians in city schools. Now there are 11—for 218 schools" (Graham 2015). In April 2015 the State School Board in Ohio voted to eliminate the "5 of 8" rule which set the minimum number of librarians, nurses, counselors, and arts teachers that school districts are required to have, at least five of eight of these positions for each 1,000 students (O'Donnell 2015). Supporters of these staff positions predict that, without the 5 of 8 mandate, particularly in difficult budget times, these positions will be the first eliminated.

In Indiana and other states, one librarian may cover multiple schools with the library either closed or staffed by a paraprofessional or parent volunteer on days that the librarian is in another school. Obviously a librarian who is not present or who is present only one day a week cannot make the same impact on student learning that a full-time, credentialed librarian can. A librarian who has adequate support staff to assist with day-to-day library operations can make an even greater difference.

According to the 2012 study, *How Pennsylvania School Libraries Pay Off: Investments in Student Achievement and Academic Standards*, "there's no substitute for a full-time, certified school librarian who's fully engaged in the teaching and learning process. Key findings include:

- "With a full-time librarian, students are more likely to score 'Advanced' and less likely to score 'Below Basic' on reading and writing tests.
- "Consistently, reading scores are better for elementary, middle, and high school students who have full-time certified librarians. In schools with full-time librarians, 'Below Basic' scores not only improve, but improve more from elementary to middle to high school as well.
- "The proportional difference in 'Advanced' reading scores associated with a full-time librarian grows from elementary to middle to high school.
- "Students who are Hispanic and whose full-time librarians have support staff are three times as likely to earn 'Advanced' writing scores as their counterparts whose full-time librarians lack such support staff" (Kachel and Lance 2013).

As the research demonstrates, school librarians make a difference in student learning. Portland (Oregon) Public Schools, which currently has a half-time library assistant in each of its schools, has allocated funds to have libraries "open for the full school day to provide library services, and . . . a teacher-librarian there at least half the time in order to provide the instructional program essential for 21st century learning" (Barack 2015b). Beaverton (Oregon) School District has added "15 new library instructional technology teacher (LITT) positions to its staff for the 2015–16 school year," reinstating positions cut several years ago (Barack 2015a).

These are steps in the right direction. Libraries staffed half-time by a certified librarian are better than libraries maintained solely by assistants or volunteers. Yet, as one of the parents who strongly advocated for librarian position reinstatement in Beaverton noted,

> Families whose children hadn't worked with professional media specialists since those positions were cut didn't know what they were missing . . . "What we realized is when you go [for] three years without a teacher librarian, new families don't know what they're advocating for," says Prochovnic, whose children are entering eighth and 11th grade this fall. "Kids still come home with books because the library media assistants are doing those functions amazingly well" (Barack 2015a).

Library assistants check books in and out. Full-time certified librarians function as teachers, instructional partners, information specialists, instructional leaders, and program administrators. Efforts have been made in the past and are ongoing to include language requiring a state-certified librarian in every school, the Strengthening Kids' Interest in Learning and Libraries Act or the SKILLS Act, as part of the reauthorization of the Elementary and Secondary Education Act of 1965 (S.312 SKILLS Act 2015). Every child deserves the services of a full-time, credentialed school librarian.

FILTERS AND ACCESS

Even if you have a full-time librarian in your school, however, other factors may limit the impact that she can have on student learning. The Children's Internet Protection Act (CIPA), enacted by Congress in 2000, requires that schools filter Internet access in order to receive discounted Internet access through the E-rate program (FCC 2014). Depending on the filtering system in place, appropriate Internet sites and even information in subscription databases may be blocked. Students doing research on "breast cancer" or "gun control," for example, may find that they are unable to access many legitimate sites due to unnecessarily restrictive blocking.

Similarly, school district policies may limit access to information and subsequently limit the librarian's teaching effectiveness. It is difficult to teach digital citizenship if all social media tools are blocked by the school district. If students are not able to blog, for example, they are not able to develop the skill of appropriately commenting on others' posts. If all YouTube access is blocked, the opportunity is lost to teach valuable media literacy skills.

With the increase of allowed personal devices in schools and the implementation of Bring Your Own Device (BYOD) initiatives, teaching opportunities abound. While on school grounds, are students required to use the school network instead of their own personal access? This presents an opportunity to emphasize appropriate use of network services and honoring signed acceptable use agreements. No such restriction in place? This presents the perfect opportunity to discuss digital citizenship, privacy issues, and cyberbullying. Twenty-first-century school librarians embrace teachable moments.

Another challenge, however, that many school librarians face is an inadequate number of computers or devices to use for instruction. The librarian who only has five computers or iPads in the library can be creative, perhaps setting up stations. One station will involve the use of the computers or devices; a second may involve working with print reference sources such as almanacs and atlases, while a third may require students to work with informational texts from the general library collection.

For some instructional activities, however, every student needs to be engaged hands-on on the computer or device. An inadequate number of computers in the library, or a lab or laptop/iPad cart that is always in use for test preparation or testing limits what the librarian can accomplish instructionally with students. Access to technology is critical if the librarian is to integrate technology into instruction and provide authentic learning experiences for the students.

Challenges to full utilization of the skills of 21st-century school librarians, therefore, lie in previous perceptions or lack of awareness of what librarians can do, librarians who themselves have not fully embraced their instructional roles, lack of staffing since it is not possible to utilize what you do not have, and filters and district policies that unnecessarily restrict access to information and the librarian's teaching effectiveness. What then are the benefits of tapping into the skills of the 21st-century school librarian?

BENEFITS

Performance-Based Evaluation

Various documents exist to guide evaluation of school librarians, among them AASL's 2010 "Sample Job Description, Title: School Librarian" (see appendix B) and *A 21st-Century Approach to School Librarian Evaluation* (AASL 2012), but with Race to the Top and No Child Left Behind waivers, states are required to implement performance-based evaluations that demonstrate student academic progress (Pennington 2014, 1). Tapping into the skills of the 21st-century librarian who takes an active part in the instructional program of the school should make the entire performance-based evaluation process simpler.

As you are working to evaluate the school librarian, you now know what to expect, what to look for, and what to document regarding performance. The librarian's job goes beyond that of the classroom teacher as she establishes a culture of inquiry and learning in the library, provides a collection of resources to support informational and instructional needs, promotes books and reading, and collaborates with teachers to integrate technology and various library information skills into classroom content instruction. More importantly, she teaches.

Whatever the term used in your state or district—student learning outcomes, student growth measures, student achievement goals, student academic progress—librarians must be able to document that they positively impact student learning through instruction in the library. This instruction and documentation is not without challenges, however: in a 2013 survey of Virginia school librarians, while 67 percent of respondents indicated that they had adequate cooperation from classroom teachers, only 40 percent felt that they had adequate contact time with students to instruct and assess (Church 2015). Librarians must have sufficient access to the students in order to teach them.

With access to the students and cooperation from and collaboration with the classroom teacher, the librarian can document an instructional need, measure students' current knowledge, set learning objectives, teach, and evaluate student progress. Successful implementation of this process allows for student learning, building collaborative partnerships, and collection of data needed for the student academic progress portion of the performance-based evaluation.

Professional Learning Community

When the skills of 21st-century school librarians are fully utilized, a side benefit is the development of a collaborative, professional learning community within the school. The library serves as the learning commons, a place where ideas and information are freely exchanged. The librarian serves as professional developer, providing relevant in-house professional development which then allows for scaffolding and reinforcement following the actual professional development workshop or session. The librarian models collaboration with classroom teachers and technology specialists, which fosters further collaborative efforts, and a collaborative culture is established.

Maximized Student Learning

The ultimate benefit of full utilization of the skills of the 21st-century school librarian, of course, is maximized student learning. "Quality school library programs impact student achievement. Since the 1990s when standardized tests became a major indicator of student learning, numerous studies have been conducted to confirm the educational gains that school library programs provide in student learning. The most universal finding is the presence of full-time, certified school librarians and appropriate support staff who implement a quality, school-integrated program of library services" (Kachel 2013, 4).

When librarians are actively involved in teaching, test scores increase. Even more important than the test scores, though, is student learning as demonstrated in preparation for college and career through authentic learning experiences. Librarians teach students to access information efficiently, to evaluate information critically, and to use information competently. They teach students to think critically, to problem-solve, and to communicate effectively. They empower students with useful skills for lifelong learning.

IN SUMMARY: CHALLENGES AND BENEFITS

Tapping into the skills of 21st-century school librarians presents various challenges, but these challenges are greatly outweighed by the benefits to the overall school culture and to student learning. Full utilization of the librarians' skills will reap tremendous rewards.

ADDITIONAL READINGS

Kuon, Tricia, and Holly Weimar. 2012. "How Does Your Boss See You?" *School Library Journal* 58, no. 9: 36–39.

The authors share the results of a survey of school librarians and principals, addressing the use of technology, promotion of recreational reading, and school librarians as leaders.

Moreillon, Judi. 2013. "Leadership: School Librarian Evaluation." *School Library Monthly* 30, no. 2, 24–25.

Moreillon discusses performance-based evaluation for school librarians and suggests that this is an opportunity for librarians to demonstrate a measurable difference in student learning.

Purcell, Melissa. 2010. "All Librarians Do Is Check Out Books, Right? A Look at the Roles of a School Library Media Specialist." *Library Media Connection* 29, no. 3: 30–33.

Purcell discusses the five roles of a 21st-century school librarian and duties performed in each.

REFERENCES

Alexander, Linda B., Robert. C. Smith, and James O. Carey. 2003. "Education Reform and the School Library Media Specialist." *Knowledge Quest* 32, no. 2: 10–13.

American Association of School Librarians. 2009. *Empowering Learners: Guidelines for School Library Programs*. Chicago: American Library Association.

American Association of School Librarians. 2010. "Sample Job Description, Title: School Librarian." Accessed July 6, 2015. http://www.ala.org/aasl/sites/ala.org.aasl/files/content/guidelinesandstandards/learning4life/resources/sample_job_description_L4L.pdf

American Association of School Librarians. 2012. *A 21st-Century Approach to School Librarian Evaluation*. Chicago: American Library Association.

Barack, Lauren. 2015a. "Beaverton (OR) Green-Lights 15 New Teacher Librarian Positions." Accessed July 6, 2015. http://www.slj.com/2015/06/budgets-funding/beaverton-or-greenlights-15-new-teacher-librarian-positions/

Barack, Lauren. 2015b. "Portland (OR) Public Schools to School Librarians: We Want You!" Accessed July 6, 2015. http://www.slj.com/2015/06/budgets-funding/portland-or-public-schools-to-school-librarians-we-want-you/

Bernstein, Allison. 2011. "The Big Elephant in the Library." *Library Media Connection* 30, no. 3: 46.

Church, Audrey P. 2008. "The Instructional Role of the Library Media Specialist As Perceived by Elementary School Principals." *School Library Media Research*, 11. Accessed July 4, 2015. http://www.ala.org/aasl/aaslpubsandjournals/slmrb/slmrcontents/volume11/church

Church, Audrey P. 2010. "Secondary School Principals' Perceptions of the School Librarian's Instructional Role." *School Library Research*, 13. Accessed July 4, 2015. http://www.ala.org/aasl/sites/ala.org.aasl/files/content/aaslpubsandjournals/slr/vol13/SLR_SecondarySchool_V13.pdf

Church, Audrey P. 2015. "Performance-Based Evaluation and School Librarians." *School Library Research*, 18. Accessed July 6, 2015. http://www.ala.org/aasl/sites/ala.org.aasl/files/content/aaslpubsandjournals/slr/vol18/SLR_PerformanceBasedEvaluation_V18.pdf

Federal Communications Commission. 2014. "Children's Internet Protection Act." Accessed July 6, 2015. https://www.fcc.gov/guides/childrens-internet-protection-act

Graham, Kristen A. 2015. "School Cuts Have Decimated Librarians." Philly.com. Accessed July 5, 2015. http://articles.philly.com/2015-02-02/news/58679838_1_school-library-librarian-philadelphia-school-district

Hartzell, Gary. 2002. "The Principal's Perceptions of School Libraries and Teacher-Librarians." *School Libraries Worldwide* 8, no. 1: 92–110.

Hartzell, Gary. 2012. "Why Doesn't School Library Impact Research Have More Influence on School Leaders? Implications for Advocacy: An Opinion Piece." *Library Media Connection*. Accessed July 4, 2015. http://www.librarymediaconnection.com/pdf/lmc/reviews_and_articles/featured_articles/Hartzell_October2012.pdf

Kachel, Debra E. 2013. "School Library Research Summarized: A Graduate Class Project." Revised ed. Accessed July 6, 2015. http://sl-it.mansfield.edu/upload/MU-LibAdvoBklt2013.pdf

Kachel, Debra E., and Keith Curry Lance. 2013. "Latest Study: A Full-time School Librarian Makes a Critical Difference in Boosting Student Achievement." Accessed July 6, 2015. http://www.slj.com/2013/03/research/librarian-required-a-new-study-shows-that-a-full-time-school-librarian-makes-a-critical-difference-in-boosting-student-achievement/#_

Kaplan, Allison G. 2006. "Benign Neglect: Principals' Knowledge of and Attitudes towards School Library Media Specialists." Diss. University of Delaware. Accessed July 4, 2015. ProQuest (3220729).

Lofton, Jane. 2015. "Why Do We Need Teacher-Librarians?" *The CUE Blog*. Accessed July 5, 2015. http://blog.cue.org/why-do-we-need-teacher-librarians/

O'Donnell, Patrick. 2015. "State School Board Vote Eliminates Minimum Number of School Nurses, Librarians, Counselors, Arts Teachers." Accessed July 5, 2015. http://www.cleveland.com/metro/index.ssf/2015/04/breaking_state_school_board_vote_eliminates_minimum_number_of_school_nurses_librarians_counselors_arts_teachers.html

Pennington, Kaitlin. 2014. *ESEA Waivers and Teacher-Evaluation Plans: State Oversight of District-Designed Teacher-Evaluation Systems*. Washington, DC: Center for American Progress. Accessed July 6, 2015. https://cdn.americanprogress.org/wp-content/uploads/2014/05/TeacherEvalWaivers-FINAL.pdf

S.312 SKILLS Act. 2015. Accessed July 5, 2015. https://www.congress.gov/bill/114th-congress/senate-bill/312

Valenza, Joyce Kasman, and Doug Johnson. 2009. "Things That Keep Us Up at Night." *School Library Journal* 55, no. 10: 28–32.

Veltze, Linda L. 1992. "School library media program information in the principalship preparation program." In J. B. Smith and J. G. Coleman Jr. (eds.), *School Library Media Annual 1992*, vol. 10, 129–34. Englewood, CO: Libraries Unlimited.

Virginia Department of Education. 2014. "2014 Standards of Quality: §§ 22.1-253.13:1 through 22.1-253.13:10 of the Code of Virginia." Accessed January 18, 2015. www.doe.virginia.gov/administrators/superintendents_memos/2014/183-14a.pdf

Wilson, Patricia Potter, and Angus J. McNeil. 1998. "In the Dark: What's Keeping Principals from Understanding Libraries?" *School Library Journal* 44, no. 9: 114–16.

7

FINAL THOUGHTS: YOU HAVE THE POWER!

Through the years researchers have studied such topics as interactions between principals and librarians, principals' perceptions of librarians, and principals' understanding of the work a school librarian does. In the review of literature for her study of South Carolina principals, Donna Shannon (2009) suggested "one consistent finding across studies indicates that principals consider activities related to materials provision and reference assistance to be more important than collaboration, planning with teachers, and curriculum development" (2).

Seemingly, times are changing. In Shannon's own study (2009) principals rated the following two competencies of school librarians most highly: "Collaborates with teachers to provide students with instruction in strategies such as finding, judging, and using information in support of active, authentic learning" and "Collaborates with teachers to integrate the library program and information literacy skills into the school's curriculum" (7–8).

Exploring the perceptions of librarians and administrators in a Louisiana public school district, Kira Berggren (2013) found "that not only did administrators and school librarians share similarities in their perceptions with regard to the professional roles, but they also agreed on various reasons for identifying school librarians as additional educational leaders" (iv). Acknowledgment of librarians as instructional leaders in their schools is a tremendous endorsement of the key role they play.

Kuon and Weimar (2012) found that principals rate the librarian's top three tasks as "Help students to access information and books; Help faculty to access information and books; and Share technology expertise with students and teachers." "Collaborate with teachers" was number six on the list, "Provide leadership with technology" was number eight, and "Teach research skills, teach about books, and teach about databases" was number nine. All of these are tasks librarians complete as teachers, instructional partners, information specialists, instructional leaders, and program administrators.

In a recent *Connected Principals* blog post (2015), Todd Samuelson, school administrator in a grade 7 to 12 Alberta, Canada, school, described the partnership that he has with his teacher-librarian, discussing the transition from traditional library to library learning commons and the impact that it has had on student learning. "Our Learning Commons has helped shift the culture of the school. Its presence in the building and its focus on students, learning, wellness, technology, and collaboration all spill into the rest of the school." He describes his librarian as "a capacity-builder, innovator, risk taker, master teacher and learning leader" (Samuelson 2015).

Throughout this book, the multiple roles of a 21st-century school librarian have been explored and explained: teacher, instructional partner, information specialist, instructional leader, and program administrator. In practice in a 21st-century school library, the roles are interconnected and intertwined. With a strong program in place, the librarian is viewed as a leader within the school as she utilizes information resources to teach collaboratively with fellow teachers.

AND IF YOU HAVE THE OPPORTUNITY TO HIRE?

David Loertscher in his "Principal's Taxonomy of Library Media Programs" suggests that, at level three, the "administrator attracts a library media specialist to head the program who has the vision and energy to create and maintain a solid LMC program" (2000, 58). (See the complete principal taxonomy in appendix C.) Today's 21st-century school librarian has vision and energy as well as the skills needed to create such a program.

Consider the following May 25, 2015, blog post from Jennifer La-Garde, aka Library Girl, reprinted here with permission:

Dear Principal,

I know you're busy, so I won't mince words: Hiring and supporting awesome people to work with the students who go to your school is the most important part of your job. Period. It's not school safety. It's not community outreach. It's not busses, instructional services or building maintenance. It's people. Because the better people you have, the more empowered and capable they are, the fewer problems you'll have in all of those other areas. Great people = great outcomes.

That said, I'm willing to bet you spend a lot of time thinking about this. Especially at this time of year when resumes, resignations, transfers and retirements start coming in. As a lifelong teacher, I associate the end of any school year with lots of things: kids waving out of bus windows for the last time, empty lockers, quiet hallways and an almost indescribable exhaustion. But for the principal, this time of year also means looking for and hiring new people.

In my experience most principals have developed a pretty good system for hiring new classroom teachers. They have a team of go to instructional leaders to serve on the committee, a list of finely tuned questions to ask and enough gut instinct to know when they've found "the one." When it comes to hiring new school librarians, however, the process is often a little less efficient.

And look, that's not your fault. I get it. Chances are, you've a) never been a school librarian, b) never hired a school librarian, c) never collaborated with a school librarian (back when you were a classroom teacher) and d) you probably also missed that nonexistent lecture in principal school in which you were told what to expect from the school librarian you would soon supervise. But despite the lack of guidance you've received in this area, trust me, this is important. As important as hiring a new 5th, 8th or 11th grade teacher. In some ways, *more important*, because your school librarian will work with every teacher and every student in your building. She will purchase materials that support both your core curriculum and the interventions you design for your most vulnerable students. He will lead the way in technology initiatives and build the programs that help develop the literacy habits of your little learners. This is a big and important job. And you need someone who is up to the task. You need an awesome librarian.

And I am going to help you find one.

As you prepare to interview and select candidates for this role, here's what you do:

1. *Look for someone who loves children more than books.* Books are awesome. And your new librarians should love them. But they should love children more. Look for passion when you talk to them about their job, but make sure that passion revolves around what makes being a school librarian the best job in the world: the opportunity to match kids with the first book to change their lives.

2. *Look for the right person as opposed to the right degree.* Librarians reading about this are not going to like this suggestion, but the right person can earn the right degree later. That transformation rarely works in reverse, however. Besides, I'll tell you a little secret. I wasn't finished with my degree when a principal took a chance on me as a fledgling school librarian. And I turned out okay. (I want to be clear. You NEED a certified, degreed, school librarian. But if you find the right person who is willing to get that degree and certification, and your system allows you to hire such candidates, don't let their initial lack of credentialing stand in the way of hiring someone who is awesome.)

3. *Look for data and outcomes.* Data comes in all shapes and sizes. Ask how your potential new school librarian uses it to make sure her work matters. Find out what kinds of data she collects, how she changes her practice to meet individual student needs and how she uses it to evaluate the effectiveness of her work.

4. *Look for someone who can grow readers, not just reading scores.* Developing reading skills and developing the habit of reading are two different things. But when we talk about the important work of helping students thrive (and achieve), one thing cannot exist without the other. You need a school

librarian who can support the work of classroom teachers while also creating spaces, events, instruction and programming that help make reading an essential part of your students' lives.

5. *Look for a leader (or one in training).* I've said it before, but it's worth repeating, your school librarian works with every student and every teacher in your school. You need a coach, a cheerleader, a visionary, a risk taker and a rebel. You need someone who is willing to do whatever it takes for your students and who will inspire others to do the same.

6. *Look for a learner.* Ask them about their habits as a learner. Ask them who their instructional heroes are, where they go for pedagogical inspiration and how they continue to grow as a practitioner of the world's most important art. Look for someone for whom learning is a part of their DNA, because only a "lifelong learner" can model that passion for someone else.

But that's not all. Finding the right person is only part of the equation. Once you've hired the perfect candidate, they are going to need you to do a few things to help them be the very best school librarian they can be. You have to support them. And here's how:

1. *Have high expectations.* In my experience, people rise and fall to the expectations that are set for them. So set your expectations high and watch your new school librarian rise. That said . . .

2. *Give them meaningful work.* Providing other teachers with a planning period is not meaningful work. Forcing students to select books within a certain Lexile band is not meaningful work. Checking books in and out all day long is not meaningful work. Give them important work. Work that matters. To whatever extent possible, give them time to collaborate with classroom teachers, manage your school's collection of resources and work with students in ways that produce real outcomes.

3. *Put your money where your priorities are.* Over and over again, studies show that sufficiently and consistently funded school library programs positively impact student achievement. And I know, these are lean times. You won't be given enough money to fund all the programs you'd like, but an investment in your library program is an investment in your students. Ask yourself how much that's worth to you and then allot accordingly.

4. *Be present. Be proud.* Visit the library as often as you can and show off the great work being done there. When prospective parents, school board members or the superintendent stop by for a visit, make sure your school library is a stop on the tour. Together, you and your librarian are going to build something awesome. Be sure to show it off.

I know. That's a lot. But you can do it. . . .

Now . . . go forth and find the school librarian your students deserve.

Love,

Library Girl

LaGarde's advice is sound. If you have the opportunity to hire a librarian—your current librarian retires or you are in a situation where librarian positions are being reinstated—embrace the opportunity to hire a librarian with vision and energy who will implement the roles described in this book. Everyone in your school community—students, teachers, parents, community members—will be the better for it.

If your librarian is not performing as teacher, instructional partner, information specialist, instructional leader, and program administrator, you now know what to expect. Examine what you are doing to support her and the library program in the school, and use this book as a conversation starter. Great potential exists.

If you currently have a librarian who displays the skills and fulfills the roles described here, you realize the valuable asset that she is to your school, your faculty, and your students. You have tapped into those skills, and you have provided the necessary support. Strong school librarians positively impact student learning, and you have the power to make it happen!

REFERENCES

Berggren, Kira Chauvin. 2013. "The Professional Roles of 21st-Century School Librarians: A Mixed-Methods Study of the Perceptions of Administrators and School Librarians in a Louisiana Public School District." Ed.D. diss., Southeastern Louisiana University. ProQuest (3602475).

Kuon, Tricia, and Holly Weimar. 2012. "How Does Your Boss See You?: Proof That Principals Value Librarians." Accessed July 6, 2015. http://www.slj.com/2012/09/industry-news/how-does-your-boss-see-you-proof-that-principals-value-librarians/

LaGarde, Jennifer. 2015. "An Open Letter to Principals (Before You Hire a New School Librarian)." *Adventures of Library Girl.* Accessed July 6, 2015. http://www.librarygirl.net/2015/05/an-open-letter-to-principals-before-you.html

Loertscher, David V. 2000. *Taxonomies of the School Library Media Program.* 2nd ed. San Jose, CA: HiWillow.

Samuelson, Todd. 2015. "The Teacher-Librarian/Administrator Relationship." *Connected Principals.* Accessed July 6, 2015. http://connectedprincipals.com/archives/11623

Shannon, Donna M. 2009. "Principals' Perspectives of School Librarians." *School Libraries Worldwide* 15, no. 2: 1–22.

Appendix A

LIST OF STATE VIRTUAL LIBRARIES

State	Library	URL
Alabama	AVL: Alabama Virtual Library	http://www.avl.lib.al.us/
Alaska	Alaska State Library	http://library.alaska.gov/
Arizona	Arizona State Library	http://www.azlibrary.gov/
Arkansas	Traveler	http://www.asl.lib.ar.us/traveler/index.html
California	California State Library	http://www.library.ca.gov/
Colorado	Colorado State Library	http://www.cde.state.co.us/cdelib/
Connecticut	ICONN	http://www.iconn.org
Delaware	Delaware Library Catalog	http://delaware.lib.overdrive.com/327F1435-0DD6-4601-A450-D3329B91B489/10/50/en/Default.htm
Florida	Florida Electronic Library	http://flelibrary.org/
Georgia	GALILEO	http://www.galileo.usg.edu
Hawaii	Hawaii State Public Library System	http://www.librarieshawaii.org/Serials/databases.html
Idaho	LiLI	http://www.lili.org/
Illinois	Find It! Illinois!	http://www.finditillinois.org/tryit/
Indiana	INSPIRE	http://www.inspire.net/
Iowa	Iowa Library Services/State Library	http://www.statelibraryofiowa.org/ld/databases
Kansas	Kansas State Library	http://kslib.info/
Kentucky	KY Virtual Library	http://www.kyvl.org/
Louisiana	Louisiana Library Connection	http://lalibcon.state.lib.la.us/
Maine	MARVEL	http://libraries.maine.edu/mainedatabases/
Maryland	Sailor	http://www.sailor.lib.md.us/
Massachusetts		http://mblc.state.ma.us/index.php
Michigan	Library of Michigan	www.michigan.gov/libraryofmichigan
Minnesota	ELM	http://elm4you.org/
Mississippi	MAGNOLIA	http://library.msstate.edu/magnolia/
Missouri	Missouri State Library	http://s1.sos.mo.gov/library
Montana	MLN	http://home.msl.mt.gov/
Nebraska	NebraskaAccess	http://www.nlc.state.ne.us/nebraskaccess/index.html
Nevada	CLAN	http://www.clan.lib.nv.us/Polaris/
New Hampshire	NHewLINK	http://www.nhewlink.state.nh.us/schools/index.html
New Jersey	New Jersey State Library	http://www.njstatelib.org/
New Mexico	New Mexico State Library	http://nmstatelibrary.org/
New York	NOVEL	http://novelnewyork.org/
North Carolina	WISE OWL	http://www.ncwiseowl.com/
North Dakota	North Dakota State Library	http://www.library.nd.gov/index.html
Ohio	INFOHIO	http://www.infohio.org/
Oklahoma	Digital Prairie	http://www.odl.state.ok.us/prairie/index.htm

Oregon	OSLIS	http://oslis.org/
Pennsylvania	POWER	http://www.powerlibrary.net/
Rhode Island		http://sos.ri.gov/library/
South Carolina	DISCUS	http://www.scdiscus.org/index.html
South Dakota	South Dakota State Library	http://www.sdstatelibrary.com/
Tennessee	TSLA	http://access.gale.com/tel2/
Texas	TSLAC	https://www.tsl.texas.gov/
Utah	Pioneer	http://pioneer-library.org/
Vermont		http://libraries.vermont.gov/
Virginia	FindItVa	http://www.finditva.com
Washington	WA State Library	http://www.sos.wa.gov/library/Default.aspx
West Virginia	West VA State Archives and Libraries	http://statearchives.us/west-virginia.htm
Wisconsin	BadgerLink	http://www.badgerlink.net/
Wyoming	GoWYLD	http://gowyld.net/dbases.html

Appendix B

SAMPLE JOB DESCRIPTION, TITLE: SCHOOL LIBRARIAN

An initiative of the American Association of School Librarians

SAMPLE JOB DESCRIPTION
Title: SCHOOL LIBRARIAN

Qualifications:

- A master's degree from a program accredited by the American Library Association (or from a master's level program in library and information studies accredited or recognized by the appropriate national body of another country) is the appropriate professional degree for school librarians.

- A highly qualified candidate will also hold appropriate state certification as a school librarian and have completed a teacher preparation program and/or educational degree.

Reports To: School library supervisor/department head* and building principal

Supervises: Paraprofessional(s) who comprise the school library staff, and, if applicable, volunteers and student assistants

Job Goals: To ensure that students and staff are effective users of ideas and information

To empower students to be critical thinkers, enthusiastic readers, skillful researchers, and ethical users of information

To instill a love of learning in all students and ensure equitable access to information

To collaborate with classroom teachers and specialists to design and implement lessons and units of instruction, and assess student learning and instructional effectiveness

To provide the leadership and expertise necessary to ensure that the school library program (SLP) is aligned with the mission, goals, and objectives of the school and the school district, and is an integral component of the learning/instructional program

ROLES AND RESPONSIBILITIES

Leader

As a leader the school librarian creates an environment where collaboration and creative problem solving thrive. The school librarian is an excellent communicator who instills enthusiasm in others by making them feel that they are important members of a team. Strong leaders foster an environment of creativity, innovation, and openness to new ideas, welcoming and encouraging input from others to create consensus. They anticipate future obstacles and continually retool to meet challenges. The school librarian demonstrates his or her role as a visible and active leader within the school community, an advocate for the SLP, and a professional member of the school library community by:

- serving on decision making teams in the school

- taking an active role in school improvement and accreditation activities

- benchmarking the SLP to school, state, and national program standards

- sharing expertise by presenting at faculty meetings, parent meetings, and school board meetings

2010 American Association of School Librarians

- creating an environment that is conducive to active and participatory learning, resource-based instructional practices, and collaboration with teaching staff

- sharing with the learning community collaboratively developed and up-to-date district policies concerning such issues as materials selection, circulation, reconsideration of materials, copyright, privacy, and acceptable use

- encouraging the use of instructional technology to engage students and to improve learning, providing 24/7 access to digital information resources for the entire learning community

- collecting and analyzing data to improve instruction and to demonstrate correlations between the SLP and student achievement

- maintaining active memberships in professional associations

- remaining current in professional practices and developments, information technologies, and educational research applicable to school library programs

- advocating for school library programs and the guiding principles of the school library profession; the school librarian is an active, accessible, and informed proponent of the school library profession by:

    o advocating, communicating, and promoting opportunities to improve the profession

    o maintaining frequent and timely communication to stakeholders through the school and library website, parent newsletter, e-mail, and other formats, such as local cable access television, video/audio streaming, and on-demand video/podcasts

    o using local, state, national, and international school library data and research to engage support

    o writing articles and submitting regular reports providing evidence of what the library and school librarian do to prepare learners to be successful in the twenty-first century

    o maintaining an effective public relations program

    o demonstrating a commitment to maintaining intellectual freedom

    o promoting the ethical use of information

Instructional Partner
As an instructional partner the school librarian works with teachers and other educators to build and strengthen connections between student information and research needs, curricular content, learning outcomes, and information resources. The school librarian demonstrates his or her role as an essential and equal partner in the instructional process by:

- participating in the curriculum development process at both the building and district level to ensure that the curricula include the full range of literacy skills (information, media, visual, digital, and technological literacy) necessary to meet content standards and to develop lifelong learners

- collaborating with teachers and students to design and teach engaging inquiry and learning experiences and assessments that incorporate multiple literacies and foster critical thinking

- participating in the implementation of collaboratively planned learning experiences by providing group and individual instruction, assessing student progress, and evaluating activities

- joining with teachers and others to plan and implement meaningful experiences that will promote a love of reading and lifelong learning

- providing and planning professional development opportunities within the school and district for and with all staff, including other school librarians

2010 American Association of School Librarians

Information Specialist

As information specialist, the school librarian provides leadership and expertise in the selection, acquisition, evaluation, and organization of information resources and technologies in all formats, as well as expertise in the ethical use of information. The school librarian ensures equitable access and responsible use of information by:

- in accordance with district policy, developing and maintaining a collection of resources appropriate to the curriculum, the learners, and the teaching styles and instructional strategies used within the school community

- cooperating and networking with other libraries, librarians, and agencies to provide access to resources outside the school

- modeling effective strategies for developing multiple literacies

- evaluating, promoting, and using existing and emerging technologies to support teaching and learning, supplement school resources, connect the school with the global learning community, communicate with students and teachers, and provide 24/7 access to library services

- providing guidance in software and hardware evaluation, and developing processes for such evaluation

- understanding copyright, fair use, and licensing of intellectual property, and assisting users with their understanding and observance of the same

- organizing the collection for maximum and effective use

Teacher

As a teacher, the school librarian empowers students to become critical thinkers, enthusiastic readers, skillful researchers, and ethical users of information. The school librarian supports students' success by guiding them in:

- reading for understanding, for exposure to diversity of viewpoints and genres, and for pleasure

- using information for defined and self-defined purposes

- building on prior knowledge and constructing new knowledge

- embracing the world of information and all its formats

- working with peers in successful collaboration for learning

- constructively assessing their own learning and the work of their peers

- becoming their own best critics

Program Administrator

As program administrator, the school librarian works collaboratively with members of the learning community to define the policies of the school library program, and to guide and direct all activities related to it. The school librarian maximizes the efficiency and effectiveness of the school library program by:

- using strategic planning for the continuous improvement of the program

- ensuring that school library program goals and objectives are aligned with school and district long-range strategic plans

- using effective management principles, including the supervision of personnel, resources, and facilities, in developing and implementing program goals and objectives

2010 American Association of School Librarians

- using evidence of practice, particularly in terms of learning outcomes, to support program goals and planning

- generating evidence in practice that demonstrates efficacy and relevance of the school library instructional program

- conducting ongoing action research and evaluation that creates data that is used to inform continuous program improvement

- supervising and evaluating support staff, which may include educational assistants, computer education assistants, volunteers, and student assistants

- preparing, justifying, and administering the school library program budget to support specific program goals

- establishing processes and procedures for selection, acquisition, circulation, resource sharing, etc. that assure appropriate resources are available when needed

- creating and maintaining in the school library a teaching and learning environment that is inviting, safe, flexible, and conducive to student learning

- selecting and using effective technological applications for management purposes

- participating in the recruiting, hiring, and training of other professionals, educational library assistants, students, and volunteer staff

- arranging for flexible scheduling of the school libraries to provide student accessibility to staff and resources at point of need

- ensuring equitable physical access to school library facilities by providing barrier-free, universally designed environments.

Terms of Employment: Teacher work year plus extended-year days

Evaluation: Performance of this job will be evaluated in accordance with district policies.

* in a large district

(Adapted with permission from Londonderry (NH) School District, © 2000; revised 2007.)

Affiliate L4L Coordinator Workgroup

Sara Kelly Johns, Lake Placid (NY) Middle/High School; School Library Media Section of the New York Library Association (SLMS/NYLA)

Kathleen McBroom, Dearborn (MI) Public Schools; Michigan Association for Media in Education (MAME)

Cassandra E. Osterloh, Queen of Heaven School, Albuquerque, NM; Advocacy for School Libraries Special Interest Group of the New Mexico Library Association (ASL-SIG/NMLA)

Jane Prestebak, Robbinsdale (MN) Area Schools; Minnesota Educational Media Association (MEMO)

Appendix C

THE PRINCIPAL'S TAXONOMY OF THE LIBRARY MEDIA PROGRAM

Reprinted with permission from Dr. David V. Loertscher

1. AMBIVALENCE TOWARD OR NEGLECT OF THE LIBRARY MEDIA PROGRAM

For some reason, the concept of the LMC program is not supported by the administrator in the school, whether from lack of understanding, personnel problems, different priorities, or financial exigency.

2. ADMINISTRATOR MAKES AN EFFORT TO UNDERSTAND THE ROLE OF THE MODERN LMC IN A WORLD OF INFORMATION TECHNOLOGY

Few programs in the school have undergone as significant a change in role concept as has the program of the LMC in the age of technology. Even neglecting five years of reading the professional literature about this program would be a mistake.

3. ADMINISTRATOR ATTRACTS A LIBRARY MEDIA SPECIALIST TO HEAD THE PROGRAM WHO HAS THE VISION AND ENERGY TO CREATE AND MAINTAIN A SOLID LMC PROGRAM

Much rests on the vision and organizational skill of the person who heads the library media program in a school. The administrator works actively to employ a person who has a shared vision of the impact the LMC program can have.

4. ADMINISTRATOR CREATES A PARTNERSHIP WITH THE HEAD OF THE LMC PROGRAM AND PLACES THAT PERSON ON THE LEADERSHIP TEAM OF THE SCHOOL

Whatever leadership cadres exist in the school—curriculum committees, technology committees, grade level teams, or department chairs—the administrator sees that the library media specialist is a part of the right groups where the impact of information technology will be central to the push for excellence in education.

5. ADMINISTRATOR CREATES AN ORGANIZATIONAL STRUCTURE THAT ALLOWS THE LMC PROGRAM TO SUCCEED

Issues such as flexible access to the LMC, open hours, and security of facilities and technology systems must be handled in such a way that the LMC becomes a learning laboratory capable of contributing significantly to the educational program in every learning space within the school and on into the home.

6. ADMINISTRATOR PROVIDES LEADERSHIP IN BUILDING FINANCIAL SUPPORT OF THE LMC PROGRAM OVER THE LONG TERM

Information technology systems are seen as an essential infrastructure requiring constant financial support if it is to remain viable in the educational program.

7. WHATEVER LEADERSHIP STYLE OR INFLUENCE THE ADMINISTRATOR HAS, EACH OF THE FOUR PROGRAM ELEMENTS OF THE LMC IS EXPECTED TO CONTRIBUTE TO ACADEMIC ACHIEVEMENT

For library media programs to contribute to academic achievement, the leadership team of the school, be it a person, a site council, or a leadership team, expect the LMC to be effective in four major areas: reading, information literacy, collaborative unit planning with teachers, and enhancing learning through technology.

8. ADMINISTRATOR ASSESSES THE IMPACT OF THE LIBRARY MEDIA PROGRAM ON THE ACADEMIC ACHIEVEMENT OF THE STUDENTS IN THE SCHOOL

Enough data are flowing into the decision-making person or group to make a judgment about impact. This evaluative information may result in a continued direction along the same path, fine tuning of the program, or a total restructuring of the LMC program.

INDEX

ABOUT THE AUTHOR

Audrey P. Church is professor and coordinator of the school librarianship graduate program at Longwood University in Farmville, Virginia. Prior to coming to Longwood to teach, she worked as a K-12 building-level librarian in Lunenburg County (Virginia) Public Schools for twenty years. She is the author of numerous journal articles, several book chapters, and two books, *Leverage Your Library to Help Raise Test Scores* (Linworth 2003) and *Your Library Goes Virtual* (Linworth 2007). A frequent presenter at state and national conferences, she earned her bachelor's degree in English from Bridgewater College (Virginia), her master of science in education with a concentration in school library media from Longwood College (Virginia), and her Ph.D. in education from Virginia Commonwealth University. She is a past president of the Virginia Educational Media Association and the Virginia Educational Research Association and president-elect of the American Association of School Librarians.

Made in the USA
Middletown, DE
10 January 2017